Hillary's America

(Liberalism – Despotism & Clintonism)

By: Mark Phillips

Table of Contents

Preface

As I write this book, the 2008 presidential campaign is in full swing, and the front runner for the Democrat nomination is none other than Hillary Rodham Clinton. There have been many words used to help describe Hillary; words such as shrill, abrasive and ruthless are some of the ones that I personally prefer. I will add hubris to the list, which is a term that means excessive pride. Prior to the 2000 Senatorial elections, Hillary's professional accomplishments consisted of being a crooked lawyer in Arkansas working on the billing records for the Rose Law Firm. The Whitewater Scandal, one of many cover ups that the spin team of Bill/Hillary has had to 'fix' was Hillary at the height of her career in private practice. Whitewater consisted mainly of the Clintons and the McDougals swindling people in Arkansas by making fraudulent land deals. I supposed a crooked lawyer running for a national political office isn't in and of itself a rare occurrence, but a first lady with nothing more on her resume' than her last name running for the Senate is a first. At least most of the other crooked lawyers held lower political offices prior to running for the Senate.

It has been said that this presidential election season is the longest in history. Many candidates from both parties have been actively campaigning since early 2007. The notable exception of course is Hillary. When she ran for the seat vacated by Senator Daniel Patrick Moynihan in New York, it was not to live out her political life in the Senate. It was to get herself back in the White House as quickly as possible. Her strong political ambitions were very clear when she was first lady. Taking an active role in presidential decision making, Mrs. Clinton tried to force Hillary-Care down the Nation's throat. A socialized health care system that would have been disastrous for the nation, but that would have pleased a certain well known 'Sicko'. Something we'll see again if she is indeed elected in November 2008. It's interesting how the liberals will criticize Dick Cheney for wielding too much power as the Vice-President. Well at least his is an official office. First lady is just the woman married to the president.

Bill Clinton's presidency was also credited with huge tax hikes, bare knuckled attacks on business, a dereliction of duty as Commander-n-Chief and eviscerating our military with reckless base closures. Hillary is loathed by most of the military, and doesn't exactly enjoy huge support from veterans either. In the midst of a war against Islamo-Fascists, a Hillary presidency would destroy both retention and recruitment for the United States military. The only thing that Hillary won't bring back from Bubba's era is Monica Lewinsky. Some say that the most dangerous people in the world today are crazy Islamic radicals like Mahmoud Ahmadinejad of Iran. Actually, for America and freedom loving people everywhere, a Hillary presidency is a greater risk. Akin to England's Neville Chamberlain who let Hitler grow from a nut case with little power to a nut case with a huge army, Hillary's actions and inactions will allow the Islamo-Fascists to gain power. The same way the 8 years of inaction under Bill Clinton culminated in the attacks of September 11, 2001. In the early days, when it was very clear what Adolf Hitler was, he could have been defeated by even France's military. Inaction on behalf of the European powers lead by leftists like Chamberlain allowed Hitler to gain power and hence we had World War II. Don't think for a moment that Islamo-Fascists of today are any less of a danger to the world than the Nazis were back then. They're even more of a threat considering Iran is well on its way to having nuclear weapons. Mahmoud Ahmadinejad has stated that when Iran develops a nuclear weapon, he will wipe Israel off the face of the planet. That is not a threat to take likely. That man is dangerous and he has every intention of carrying out his threat if allowed to do so.

For the good of the nation, and freedom loving people around the world, nothing and I mean nothing would please me more than Hillary loosing her bid for the presidency in the general election. She is considered the de facto nominee for the left. Whatever Republican does win in 2008, will have the ability to run for re-election in 2012. It's harder to unseat a sitting president than to run for an open seat as is the case this go round. If she losses now, she may well be forced to wait until 2016. She'd be 68 then, and in many circles that would count against her. John McCain was asked on Larry King if at his age, he would be a one-term President. McCain would be 72 upon taking the oath of office in 2009 if elected. After teaming up with Ted Kennedy on the pro Illegal Immigration bill, McCain has bigger problems than his age hurting his presidential run.

This is a critical period in our Nation's history. We are at war with a very determined and ruthless enemy. While attempting to fight the war on terror, we are also being attacked from within. The democrat party has deevolved from the party of Harry S. Truman to a party of aged 1960's hippie radicals that suck up to every extremist group out there. Does any really thing that the man who said "the buck stops here" would take marching orders from fringe lunatic groups like the Daily Kos or MoveOn.Org? A group so leftist and disgusting that they ran a full-page article in the New York Times calling General Petraeus General "Betray Us". While the majority of the Senate voted to condemn MoveOn.Org for running such a disgustingly slanderous ad, Hillary voted with MoveOn.Org. The sad truth is that today's democrats are left wing extremists with an agenda that threatens the very fabric of our society. At the head of this dangerously radical movement is none other than Hillary Rodham Clinton. If elected President she will do her utmost to change America to meet her leftist ideals.

Many, if not most, of those who will read this book are to the right of the political middle. As such, you will undoubtedly notice that the title of my book is to point to the stark contrasts between a conservative's view of what would make American greater, and Hillary's. As a big fan of Sean Hannity, what better way to point to the stark contrasts then by changing one word from Sean's hit television show 'Hannity's America' and call the book

'Hillary's America'.

Let's look at some stark contrasts between a conservative's view of America, and Hillary's.

Hannity's America	Hillary's America
Strong National Defense	Retreat & Surrender
Tough Border Enforcement	No Border Enforcement
Sovereign Nation	Sanctuary Nation
Lower Taxes	Higher Taxes
Reduced Government Spending	More Government Spending
Private Sector Healthcare	Hillary-Care
School Vouchers (Parental Choice)	Public Schools for the Masses
Fair & Balanced	The Fairness Doctrine
Personal Responsibility & Self Reliance	Womb to the Tomb Government Programs
A God Fearing Nation	An Atheist Nation
3 Hours a Day Every Day	24/7 Hillary for 8 Years

Chapter #1

The Longest Presidential Campaign in U.S. History

An interesting question would be to ask precisely when exactly did Hillary launch her presidential campaign. Was it back in 2006 after winning her first re-election bid to her senatorial seat in New York? Was it back in 2000 when she first ran for that seat? It would have been interesting to be a fly on the wall as she was looking at a map of the United States to try and determine which state she should call home in order to run for the Senate in 2000. Actually, neither answer is correct, for Hillary has far too much lust for raw power to be satisfied with being only 1 voice in a chorus of 100. As a brief history lesson for Hillary supporters, the Clintons are actually from Arkansas and not New York.

Was it back in 1992 when she was playing the role of the dutiful wife supporting her husband's bid for the presidency, standing by her man during the Gennifer Flowers revelations? It is worth noting that she referred to herself as Hillary Clinton during the campaign, but as soon as Bubba got elected, it went right back to Hillary Rodham Clinton. During the 8-year Clinton presidency, she exercised unprecedented power as a first lady. Hillary just isn't the socialite type, hell she isn't even that likeable unless you're a Kool-aid drinking liberal. She went right to work on Hillary-Care wearing her no-nonsense sweat band. Her first real attempt at national policy making was an utter disaster. Hillary-Care was so extreme, even the Democrat controlled congress wouldn't pass it.

Was the start of her campaign back in 1978 when Bill Clinton first ran for governor of Arkansas? I don't believe so, but we're getting closer.

I believe that it was actually on October 11, 1975, when Hillary Rodham married Bill Clinton. It was at that time she hitched her political wagon to Bill's coat tails. Numerous extra martial affairs and credible accusations of rape not withstanding, as long as it was to her political benefit to stay with Bill, nothing else mattered. Her anger with Bill for the revelation of his affair with Monica Lewinsky was not from the vantage point of a wife being mad at her husband. Monica was not the first, nor the last woman (girl) that Clinton has had an affair with. It was however the one that had the most potential to cause him political difficulty. Remember, at the time, her political aspirations were tied to his, and if Bill crashed and burned, her presidential bid would have been over before it started. At the time Zipper-Gate hit the fan Hillary had been married to that two-timing pig for over 20 years. The thought of it all being a naught is what really got Hillary Rodham pissed.

Where Are the Credentials?

I want to focus on the point of how almost immediately upon Bill's swearing in as our nation's 42nd president; Hillary was placed in charge of national health care policy making. Here women's rights groups all say how women can make it on their own merits. Actually, I believe in that statement, and can point to several outstanding examples such as Condoleezza Rice. Let's be honest with ourselves here, unlike Dr. Rice who was appointed National Security Advisor, and then Secretary of State on her own merits, Hillary got her healthcare gig solely because she was married to the boss. Her Hillary-Care plan was a total flop, as is discussed in more detail in a later chapter.

What it does show is this woman's total lack of any meaningful accomplishments that warrant her to be considered a serious candidate for our nation's highest office. She was a crooked lawyer back in Arkansas, not really a strong item on a resume'. She failed miserably with Hillary-Care, thank goodness. She was elected to the Senatorial seat in New York based on her name only. Not all that different from a young Ted Kennedy running for the Senate in 1962. At least he is actually from Massechusets. New York is a liberal state, and those leftists love the Clintons. It didn't matter that she had never lived in New York, and didn't know squat about the state itself. She probably couldn't point out Albany on a state map in 2000 if she had to. She is a raw opportunist, and that Senatorial seat was ripe for the pickings.

Since arriving in the Senate in January 2001, she has not offered up even one piece of meaningful legislation – zero – zip - nada. She gives shrill speeches espousing whichever side of an issue she believes is politically advantageous at the time, and that's about it. The reasons she hasn't worked real hard in the Senate to write a serious legislation are two-fold. One, she doesn't want to risk really screwing up and hurt her aspirations for the Presidency. Secondly, she doesn't give a damn about her duties as a United States Senator. Her senatorial seat is merely a stepping stone on her walk back to the White House. Hillary believes that she is far too smart to merely be a single voice amongst 99 other Senators.

Ruthless Politician

Hillary has lashed out at the Iraqi government for its inability to bring stability to the nation, and to resolve the differences between the Sunni and the Shia. She's even called for Prime Minister al-Maliki to step down. Now, I will admit that the Iraqi government had not made the kind of progress that many Americans would like to see. With that said however, just how productive has our own Congress been since the Democrats took over in 2006! With an approval rating in the teens, the lowest in polling history, Hillary should stop throwing stones from inside that glass house of hers.

A notable lack of passing any meaningful legislation combined with continual visceral attacks on conservatives, no Democrat especially Hillary should preach to anybody on how to bring political parties together in the spirit of national unity for the greater common good. The new Iraqi government is less than 5 years old, while ours is over 230 years old. You'd think our Congress would be the model of efficiency for the Iraqi's to follow. I wouldn't call the 210th Congress a model for any government to aspire to.

In all fairness, I will say that the Clinton's are the best politicians alive today, and perhaps the best in our nation's history. I don't mean politician in the positive sense, of a sincere desire to fix some of the real challenges that we are facing as a nation today. It is not possible to make that assumption considering the policy flip/flops Hillary is becoming renowned for. She's even challenging John *'I actually did vote for the $87 billion before I voted against it'* Kerry as Chief Democrat flip flopper. Hillary voted to authorize military action against Iraq back in October 2002. America was far more united then and seeking a strong response to the September 11th attacks. She knew that hers would be a popular vote at the time. She also gave several 'strong' speeches in 2003 stating that it was the right decision to remove Saddam Hussein from power. She also stated how he had weapons of mass destruction, and was a threat to world stability. Sentiments echoed by Bill Clinton during his tenure as President by the way. Again, Hillary believed that was the politically advantageous thing for her to do at the time so she did it.

In 2007 as a presidential candidate vying for her party's nomination, she has changed her position to pander to the far left contingent of the Democrat party. The person who has been called the smartest women in the world says that she was bamboozled by President Bush. The same liberal press that says how brilliant Hillary is also tar Bush as being a total simpleton. So how did this supposedly brilliant woman get fooled so completely?

In 2007, Hillary voted against funding our troops that are in harms way in Iraq. This is not the sign of a person with the depth of seriousness to serve as Command-n-Chief during a time of war. Her voting against our military is even more stunning when you consider that in 2006 she said that she would never cut off funding for our troops. As usual, she was being the consummate politician, and displaying unparalleled chutzpah. *Flip/flop flip/flop*. Hillary has stated that the troops are invisible to President Bush, even after voting to de-fund them while in harms way. If it weren't biologically impossible, I'd say that Hillary has got balls.

Hillary will state what she believes is politically advantageous from day to day. If a poll ever showed that the majority of Americans wanted an across the board tax cut, she'd be leading the charge. OK – maybe that is a stretch. However, the point is that a lack of true core values is what is seriously troubling about many politicians, Hillary in particular. A lack of serious core beliefs combined with the raw lust for power means that their votes are poll driven. Positions should be based on core beliefs and a desire to do what is the best thing for America and not on what you believe will guarantee your continued employment as an elected politician. Proving that she will stop at nothing, when Hillary's feminism was questioned, she took to wearing a top that showed some cleavage on the floor of the Senate. Her candidacy was at the risk of being out womanized by John Edwards aka 'Silky Pony' and the 'Breck Girl'. She had to show the world that she had the real boobs. Hillary probably hasn't shown Bill that much cleavage in years. I'm sure that good ole' Bubba doesn't have any problem finding women that will give him a nice boob shot though.

The Most Ethical Administration in History

One of the issues that Clinton campaigned on in 1992 was that his would be the most ethical administration in our nation's history. Perhaps what is truly stunning about that statement is how the Clinton's can lie with such ease and sound believable. Well, believable to left wingers at least.

In actuality, the Clinton presidency was wrought with more scandals than any administration in our Nation's history. This is the man that forced sensitive topics such as extra-marital affairs and oral sex down our throats. *'Zipper Gate'* was the nickname given to the scandal of Clinton's affair with Monica. I find it stunning how women's rights groups such as the National Organization of Women were conspicuously silent during that entire affair. Apparently a married man in a position of authority having an affair with a younger woman is only an offense when the philanderer is a conservative. Even using Monica as his personal humidor didn't seem to offend NOW.

He openly lied to the American people on national television shaking his finger at us and swearing that he didn't have sexual relations with that woman, Miss Lewinsky. If it weren't for DNA evidence, Clinton's semen on Monica's blue dress, or presidue as I like to call it, he would have stood by that lie. In fact not only did women's rights group such as NOW not criticize Clinton for his numerous affairs, they actually excused his actions and supported him. Some even claimed that Bill was such a macho dude that it was no wonder women wanted to perform oral sex on him. So, now are the women's rights groups are saying that if you're a stud then screwing around on your wife is ok? The truth of the matter is that if you're a liberal, any deviant personal act that you do is ok. Bill could have banged a sheep in the Oval Office and gotten away with it.

Yet through it all, including impeachment, Clinton enjoyed a strong following amongst the vast majority of liberals. His approval ratings actually went up in certain polls after the Senate failed to remove him from office. It was obvious to anybody that Clinton had in fact committed the impeachable offenses that he was accused of. Evidence of perjury, suborning perjury and witness tampering were all obvious for the whole nation to see. However, Democrats in the Senate abdicated their Constitutional obligations by ignoring the evidence and not voting him out of office. If it weren't for that pesky Constitutional rule about Presidents only being able to serve two terms, Clinton may well have been elected a third time. This is the same man that was disbarred by the State of Arkansas. As a symbolic protest to Clinton's gross lack of any kind of respect for the rule of law and the judiciary the entire Supreme Court boycotted one of his State of the Union addresses to the Nation.

Al Gore actually missed an opportunity here. He could have taken a morale high ground and advised the President that in light of his illegal acts that either Clinton would resign or he would. If Clinton had resigned, Gore would have been the incumbent going into the 2000 elections. If Gore had resigned, he would have had much more credibility which may have won him the presidency. He did neither, and between hanging chads and loony environmentalism, Gore has effectively McCain-ed his presidential aspirations.

Illegal Chinese Campaign Contributions

Who can forget the campaign fundraising scandals of the Clinton administration of the 1990's? Millions of dollars of illegal campaign contributions from figures like John Huang who was given a sensitive job government as payback. He was made the Assistant Secretary for International Economic Affairs, a job with access to classified information. Clinton was advised against giving Huang such a position because he was considered a national security risk. Of course, the Clinton's don't give a damn about the security of our Country, and besides Huang had access to tons of money. I guess you could say that Clinton has a yen for Chinese money.

Huang bribed his way into the government and stole classified documents sending them back to China. At the height of the campaign fund raising scandal, hundreds of people either fled the country or took the 5th, including Huang, to avoid answering tough questions and facing possible criminal charges. A cover-up that according to investigators was akin to what they saw in organized crime cases. Harold Ickes was involved in fundraising for Bill Clinton and was at the heart of much of the illegal campaign cash that was raised.

Flash forward to today, Ickes is now helping Hillary with raising campaign cash for her presidential campaign, and apparently the pattern of violating federal campaign finance laws hasn't changed much. In August of 2007, it was revealed that a Chinese family name Paw had donated some $45,000 to Hillary's campaign. In fact, since 2005, the Paw family has donated $200,000 to democrat candidates. Six members of the Paw family all live together in a very modest house that is located near the San Francisco airport. According to tax records, the head of the household,

William Paw works for the United States Postal Service and makes $49,000/year. A man's who's gross annual income is $49,000 doesn't donate $45,000 to a political candidate. Well, not legally at least.

It doesn't take a genius to figure out that the Paw family is part of an illegal money laundering scheme. As I am writing this book, the story is breaking that the likely financial backer of the Paws is a man by the name of Normal Hsu. Hsu has donated over $1,000,000 to Hillary's campaign. As you can see in Appendix A, the contributions of the Paws closely time with those of Hsu. Mr. Hsu has legal problems of his own that go beyond allegations of violation campaign finance law. He was convicted of auto theft back in the early 1991 and failed to appear for sentencing. The classy guy Hsu is, he failed to so up for court in 2007 to face those charges. Liberal judges should think twice before giving bail to people like Hsu. After posting a $2,000,000 bail with cash, he went on the lamb. He has since been captured. If Hsu goes to prison, I bet Hillary's campaign contributions from the Paw family will mysteriously stop. That is of course unless the Chinese government installs another front man to funnel illegal monies through the

Paw family to Hillary.

This is yet another example in a long line of things that show that the Clintons are very corrupt, believe that they are above the law and will do anything in the name of acquiring power. In fairness, Hillary has donated $23,000 of the illegal campaign cash to charity. Of course, that does leave her with $977,000 of dirty money, but it is a start. The real risk here isn't that yet another Clinton is dealing in illegal campaign cash, it's what promises were made. What kind of job will a member of the Paw family get if Hillary is elected? How many more national security secrets do we want stolen and handed over to China?

Intellectual - Emotional

I've often said that conservatism is an intellectual based ideology, while liberalism is an emotional one. Doubt me? Try having an intellectual conversation with a liberal on any of the hot topics of the day. Try telling a liberal that maybe, just maybe there's a shadow of doubt on the topic of man caused Global Warming. Their attack will be akin to a mother bear protecting her cubs.

Liberals are emotionally tied to the Clintons. Despite his acts that repeatedly brought disgrace to the office, he enjoyed high approval ratings amongst liberals. You can't point to one serious thing that Bill Clinton accomplished during his 8 years in office. Many of the things that went right during his tenure were actually Republican initiatives taken directly out of the Contract with America. Clinton patted himself on the back for reforming welfare and balancing the federal budget. Yep – both items were Republican initiatives. In fact, Clinton vetoed numerous bills designed to reform welfare and to cut federal spending. When he finally relented, and the Republican initiatives began to succeed as conservatives knew they would, he immediately took credit as if they were his ideas.

The major contributing factor to the economic boom during Clinton's years in office was the advent of the Internet. The Internet came into its own during the 1990's, and caused an unprecedented surge in commerce. Despite the ranting of a total moron, Al Gore did not invent the Internet.

Clinton even campaigned in 1992 on giving America a middle-class tax cut. While he had no intention of cutting taxes, he knew that it was a winning policy position, especially in light of George H.W. Bush going back on his 'read my lips no new taxes' pledge. Of course, as soon as he was elected into office he passed the biggest peace time tax increase in our Nation's history.

If that man had any shame at all, he wouldn't show his two-timing lying face in public for the rest of his days. Of course while Governor of Arkansas, Clinton had so many bimbos that he used the state troopers to shuttle them back and forth. Now there's an effective use of the state's tax dollars, having government employees act as a chauffeuring service for Clinton's mistresses. Being an effective Governor was not what Clinton had in mind. His ambition was for the White House, and the State House was just a temporary stop over. Sound familiar?

Of course, the real question there is whether or not Bill Clinton's presidential aspirations came from inside, or was part of Hillary's 30-year run for that high office. It has been said that if not for Hillary, Bill would be just another dumb hick swindling people with crooked land deals. Hillary has used her association with Bill to feed her own insatiable lust for political power. She won't be happy with anything less than the presidency.

I was once asked if I thought Hillary would make a good vice-president. Considering her lust for power, and how people seem to meet with unnatural deaths when it suites the Clintons, it wouldn't be healthy to have her as VP. Constitutionally, a person can only be elected twice to the presidency, but can serve a total of 10 years. What would be going through her mind two years into her role as Vice-President? Hillary doesn't want to play second fiddle to any man. After Eisenhower had his heart attack there was a running joke that at the time Vice-President Richard Nixon would be walking with him towards the White House, and yell 'race you up the stairs Ike'. Hillary's lust for power and ruthlessness makes Nixon look like a Cub Scout. The Watergate break in is chump change compared to illegalities such as taking 700 FBI files on republicans with no warrants, no probable cause, not even reasonable suspicion. The only crime that they committed was being **Republican in Public**. A little bit of history, a 30 something Hillary was calling for Nixon to resign stating that any person that lies to the American people is unfit to be the President. I guess that for Hillary there's a big difference between the 1970's and the 1990's.

Chapter #2

The ~~United~~ Liberal States of America

There are several things that you've got to understand about liberals like Hillary Clinton. First of all, they believe that America is a bad country, and that our actions have created terrorism. That's actions of republican presidents like George Bush, and certainly not those of Jimmy Carter or Bill Clinton. They also believe that as a whole, the American people are far too stupid and incompetent to be able to run their own lives. They also believe that the causes that they are fighting for are so critical that anything they do to meet their ends is justifiable. These high level beliefs are important to explore because they go to the root of how liberals like Hillary think and why they believe that they are above the law. The ends justify the means, Niccolo' Machiavelli.

America is a Bad Country

I must say that it's hard for me even to type those words, for I thank God that I live in the United States. There's no other country on the face of the planet that I'd rather live in. In my youth I joined the military to say thank you in a small way to this great country. Many of us, especially conservatives, believe that America while certainly not perfect, is generally a very good and noble country.

Former British Prime Minister Tony Blair was asked why he thought America was such a good country. He stated that you only have to see how many people want to come to live in the United States to see what a great country it is. However, to a liberal like Hillary, America is a bad country whose actions are the root cause of terrorism and strife around the world. They often bemoan how we're hated by most Arabs countries, and even by some European countries such as France. I could really give a damn what France thinks about anything. I actually care less about offending the sensitivities about those living in Arab nations. Many are stuck living in the dark ages with a medieval view of the world. They'd be living in tents and reading by candle light if not for the technological advances of western nations mainly the United States. Name for me one invention that has come out of an Arab nation in the past 100 years. The suicide bomber jacket doesn't count because both the jacket and the bomb had already been invented. They just put the two together.

The truth is that America is the most giving country on the planet. There's not a country anywhere that we have refused to help in a time of crisis. Whether it's an earthquake, tsunami, volcanic eruption or any other natural disaster, the United States is always ready to help.

America hands out billions of dollars to countries in the name of foreign aide each and every year. In many cases these countries are no real allies of the United States. For example, we give millions of dollars every year to the Palestinians. Hamas, a terror organization, cried foul because we cut off the foreign aid to them when they were voted into power. They got mad because we didn't want to fund a known terrorist organization whose charter includes driving Israel into the sea. Hamas is not much worse than Arafat's Fattah party; they're actually just more honest and open about being a bunch of terrorists.

How much money went to actually feeding the poor living in the Palestinian territories, and how much went was spent on Kassam rockets and suicide bomber jackets. As an American tax payer, just how much money do we want to go to fund terrorism? It was plain to see right after the aftermath of the September 11, 2001 just how the Palestinians felt about the terrorist attacks. They were literally singing and dancing in the streets. They couldn't have been happier that 3,000 innocent people were just slaughtered. I guess foreign aide doesn't always bring a level of appreciation and gratitude. One of the first things on the 'to do' list of the administration of Mark Phillips is to immediately stop all foreign aid to countries that either are terrorists or that sponsor terrorism. OK – I don't have any plans to run for the Presidency, but it would be nice if the next Republican in the White House made that happen.

Liberalism Kills

Even in nations that are truly ravaged by poverty, our foreign aide provides little comfort and relief. Just as endless handouts don't help the poor in this country it doesn't help elsewhere around the world either. In many cases, the governmental incompetence and corruption that plunged a nation into poverty isn't eased by foreign aide. In most instances, the only thing that does happen with our foreign aide is that government officials are enriched, and millions of dollars are wasted. The real root cause of the poverty is the form of government itself. A hard truth is that the real way to bring prosperity to a nation is to encourage free enterprise and private sector ownership. The United States is the economic powerhouse largely as a result of the efforts of *We the People*. Free enterprise has made this country great, and not any liberal social welfare program. President Ronald Reagan said it best ... *'In our current crisis Government is not the solution to our problem, Government is the problem'.* The government take over of a product or service is almost always a total failure. Consider the mailing of packages. Which are more efficient, private sector companies such as, UPS and FedEx, or the United States Postal Service? Both UPS and FedEx were back to delivering packages in New Orleans within days and weeks after Hurricane Katrina. It took the United States Postal Services over 6 months to begin delivering mail there again.

Liberalism and unending foreign aide programs have done little to help those truly in need. In fact, in most cases, liberalism has added to the suffering. For example, we give billions in aid too many African countries. The standard of living in most of those countries is still shockingly low. Malaria, and other deadly diseases spread by insects take a horrible toll on many African nations. **D**ichloro-**D**iphenyl-**T**richloroethane, better known as DDT, is an effective pesticide that could ease much of the disease and suffering that is killing millions on the African continent. DDT has been banned for decades because it *may* cause cancer, and *may* harm wildlife. What we do know is that disease carrying insects *do* kill. Liberalism strikes again for by banning DDT, tens of millions have died needlessly in Africa.

Kill the Unborn

It has been a little over 30 years since the Supreme Court ruling on Roe v Wade. Since that time, some 40 million abortions have taken place in this country. The overwhelming majority of those 40 million were for the convenience of mother only. It just wasn't the right time to be pregnant. Liberals have a fit anytime the possibility of reversing Roe v Wade comes up. They say that reversing Roe will make abortions illegal in America. The truth is that reversing Roe will allow the states to make their own laws concerning the legality of abortions. Do you really believe that states like Massachusetts would make abortion illegal? Another truth is that there is no Constitutional right to kill your unborn child. However, female libs like Hillary don't even have enough of a maternal instinct to not want to kill unborn babies.

I wonder why liberals hold baby showers. If an unborn child is just a mass of tissue to be aborted at ANY time, what are they celebrating? Don't even get me started on the intellectual dishonesty of how liberals will fight tooth and nail to protect unborn animals such as chickens and eagles or just about anything on Earth, except the unborn human. Just like Hillary will flip/flop on an issue when it's to her advantage, liberals flip/flop here as well.

If the pregnancy is wanted, then the woman is an expected mother carrying her unborn child. If the pregnancy is unwanted, it's tissue. Reach out to a woman that has ever had a mis-carriage or had a child that was still-born, and ask if they had lost a child. There grief is real for they know the truth; that their baby has just died. There have also been cased where people have been charged with two counts of murder when killing a pregnant woman. How do liberals reconcile that? If somebody can be charged with murder for killing an unborn child, then how do they defend abortion?

The Supreme Court

One of the most lasting things that a president can do is to select nominees to the Supreme Court. Activist judges legislate from the bench, such as was the case in Roe v Wade. The Constitution does not guarantee a woman's right to kill her unborn child. While President George W. Bush is not conservative enough for many people on the right, on the whole there is agreement that he put two very qualified individuals on the Supreme Court. John Roberts and Samuel Alito are both brilliant men who understand the role of the court, and will restore a level of balance between the 3 branches of government. The ugly truth is that most liberal causes are just too extreme to be passed into law through the legislative and executive branches. After all, those guys have to get re-elected. However, federal judges are appointed for life, so they are free to legislate at will without fear of any repercussions.

On a domestic level, second only to illegal immigration, this is quite possibly the most serious issue. If Hillary is elected in 2008, she will appoint radical activist justices to the Supreme Court. Yet undocumented rights will be written into law and forced down our throats for decades. However, with the appointments of Alito and Roberts, if a Republican is elected, we have a chance to bring balance back to the courts. While I certainly don't wish harm to anybody, some of the liberals on the Supreme Court today are not in the best of health, and are likely just holding on hoping for a Hillary victory on 2008.

A Nation of Starving Poor

Consider for a moment that the vast majority of the quote unquote poor in the United States have a higher standard of living than most people around the world. Most poor people in the United States have indoor plumbing, electricity, heating and cooling, color televisions, telephones and more. These things are considered some of the basics of life in the United States. Compare that standard of living to poor people in Latin America, Europe, Russia, Africa and Asia.

Liberals decry how millions of children go to bed hungry each night due to the level of poverty we have in America. For a kid to go to be hungry in this country, their parents must be asleep at the switch. With programs such as welfare, food stamps, WIC (women – infants - children), not to mention all the religious and private sector outreach initiates that exist, how can you not find food to eat in this country? For the most part, people that are truly incompetent enough to have to rely solely on the charity of others to survive have made very self-destructive choices. I'm not talking about people that have run into a bit of bad luck and need short term assistance. In fact, providing a path to self-reliance is the compassionate conservative thing to do. I'm talking about people that use the nation's safety net as a hammock. Enabling people to continue to make self destructive choices by giving them free money isn't truly helping them. Does is help a drug addict to give them welfare checks and food stamps without first requiring them to stop taking drugs? Wouldn't a rehabilitation program be better for such a person in the long run? Once off drugs, they would have a much better chance of becoming productive themselves.

Liberal social programs such as Lyndon Johnson's The Great Society have produced a segment of country that are multi-generational welfare recipients. The programs are designed to keep people dependent by providing incentives for them not to work and not to get an education. For example, the more children that a woman has out of wedlock, the more money the government will give her. This has created a dramatic rise in the illegitimacy rates amongst the poor in this country.

An urban myth that liberals love to spread is that the CIA is covertly selling cocaine to inner-city minorities in order to destroy them. The truth is that liberal social programs have done the real damage to the poor and minorities. Illegitimacy rates are up, as are drop out rates amongst inner-city minorities. Test scores amongst minorities have been dropping steadily over the past 50 years. If Hillary really wanted to help the poor, she be sponsoring a bill in the Senate for school vouchers for all the nation's children. That's not going to happen of course, as liberals need dependent poor people as they overwhelmingly vote Democrat. They also care for more about the powerful Teachers Union than they do about actually providing a quality education for our nation's young. Interesting however that in the test cases where a school voucher system was utilized, it's always a huge success. Just how compassionate is it to damn a child to the public school system in areas such as Washington D.C.

In one of many acts of liberal hypocrisy, liberal politicians, send their children to private school at a rate that is far greater than the national average. Yes, Chelsea Clinton went to a private school as well. Apparently the same public school system that liberals fight to protect by denying us vouchers; isn't fit for their own children.

Enterprise Zones

Encouraging private-sector economic development is the best way to raise a community out of poverty. Simply put, giving companies an incentive to do business in inner-city neighborhoods. Such neighborhoods generally have a higher crime rate, so there is a certain degree of risk associated with moving there. However, tax incentives for companies to build factories and facilities in inner-city neighborhoods would help offset those risks, and create what is known as enterprise zones.

It would bring much needed employment opportunities to poor neighborhoods, allowing people to get jobs and obtain a degree of self reliance as well as the self respect that comes along with it. I wouldn't hold my breath for Hillary to sponsor a bill creating enterprise zones in poor inner-city neighborhoods anytime soon. Just the opposite, Hillary and her liberal ilk decry the evils of what they call 'corporate welfare'.

The hard economic truth is that corporations are not tax payers, they are tax collectors. Every penny that corporations have to pay in taxes, they simply pass on to you and me, the consumer, in the form of higher prices for the good and/or services that they provide.

The ~~Ugly~~ Stupid American

Liberals bank on the notion that we are nation of witless fools.

Fortunately for them, they have willing accomplices in the 'dinosaur' media, aka the liberal press. You'll never hear CNN, ABC, NBC, CBS et al or any of the liberal print media challenge liberals on any number of issues. When was the last time you heard a CNN anchor ask a liberal to comment on how the Bush tax cuts have resulted in a shortened Clinton/Gore recession and given us an economic boom that has seen the stock market nearly double since its post 9/11 lows?

Do you think CBS is going to challenge Hillary on her assertion that the entire Monica Lewinsky affair was made up by the *'vast right wing conspiracy'*? Especially considering that the facts are now out, and the entire nation knows that the affair and subsequent cover ups really did occur. What about Janet Reno firing all 93 federal prosecutors only months into Bill Clinton's first year as president. Now, as first lady, Hillary had nothing negative to say about that. She was not demanding the resignation of Janet Reno. Flash forward to Hillary the presidential candidate, and she's insisting that Attorney General Alberto Gonzalez resign or be fired for removing 8 federal prosecutors. Unlike the blanket firings under Reno, these were for cause and happened 6 years into Bush's administration. I believe the term that former Press Secretary Tony Snow used was *Arkansas Chutzpah*.

While on the topic of Bill Clinton's Attorney General, where was the outrage when her actions led to the death of 80 American citizens in Waco Texas, including women and children? For that matter, how many 6-year-old boys did Alberto Gonzalez take from relative's arms at gun point and return to Cuba? Reno accused the relatives of young Elian Gonzalez of breaking the law and used that premise to order federal agents to bust into their home and remove Elian by force. I guess that whole innocent until proven guilty thing doesn't apply to the Clintons. Guilty even after proven guilty doesn't even apply to Bill and Hillary. The Clinton's are the quintessential Teflon couple. We have millions of people that are in this country illegally, and Bill Clinton chooses a 6-year-old child to deport. A child, that had relatives that were in this country legally and willing to raise Elian. The lack of intellectual honesty on behalf of Hillary Clinton and liberals in general is just stunning.

Of course, indiscriminant firing of government employees is nothing new to Bill and Hillary. Almost immediately upon taking office in January 2003, the Clinton's fired the entire White House Travel Office and replaced them with Arkansas cronies. There were debts to pay, and the Clinton's (like all liberals) love to pay for things at the expense of others. Travel Office Director Billy Dale was the target of the Clinton attack machine investing this non-political government employee with embezzlement. He lost is career, spend his entire life's savings defending himself against trumped up phony criminal charges. Hillary was believed to be heavily involved in Travel-gate and even to lying about any role that she may have played. She was obviously just baking cookies for Chelsea.

Falling on the Sword

All across the country, the liberal media is loosing ground. The print media such as the New York Times are seeing subscription rates spirally steadily downward. Now, they can blame part of it on the advent of both television and the Internet. However, the issue that is having the most impact is their liberal bias. Despite what Hillary might say and think, the entire country is not made up of left wing extremists. The powers that be at the *Times* and other liberal newspapers are seeing their companies go broke as a result of their obvious leftist biases. Now, I'm not suggesting that the *Times* become a conservative blog, but some intellectual honesty would be nice. I find it stunning from a business perspective that these media executives are willing to see their companies go broke rather than remove the leftist biases that are ruining them.

The exact same phenomenon is happening with liberal television stations as well. While CNN, ABC, CBS, NBC and others of their liberal ilk may out number the Fox News Channel, liberal cable television are getting whipped in the ratings. Lou Dobbs is getting his clocks cleaned by shows such as The O'Reilly Factor and Hannity & Colmes. His ratings can't even compete with the 4:00Am rerun of the O'Reilly Factor much less Bill's prime time evening slot. Just as much of the country is not comprised of Kool-aid drinking liberals, we also like to hear the facts (both sides – fair & balanced) and to be informed. Hearing a CNN anchor babe drone on how Bush sucks just isn't the kind of television that may of us like to tune into. I can walk by a college campus and here that kind of non-sense anytime I want.

Another stark example of why liberal media is loosing ground is the rise and very rapid fall of Air America. While conservative talk radio is exploding across the fruited plane with personalities such as; Rush

Limbaugh, Sean Hannity, Laura Ingram, Michael Savage and more, Air America died in under a year. Rather than do some hard internal soul searching, the liberals want to destroy the competition by making it illegal.

The Fairness Doctrine would effectively end conservative talk radio as we know it today. As much as I love to listen to Rush, I couldn't listen to him, if he had to share the Golden EIB microphone with Al Franken. Liberals just hate it when they have to compete on an even playing field with conservatives. They get their heads handed to them each and every time.

Above The Law

The rules don't apply to liberals, and certainly not to the Clintons. As I am writing this book, Idaho republican Larry Craig has just resigned from the United States Senate. He was arrested in a Minneapolis airport for allegedly making inappropriate advances in a men's bathroom frequented by gays trying to meet. He was charged with giving non-verbal signals allegedly indicating that he wanted to have sex with the person in the next stall. Unfortunately for Senator Craig, the man in the next stall was an undercover police officer. Craig pleaded guilty to the misdemeanor crime of disorderly conduct. Hillary and the oh so righteous liberals were demanding an investigation and that Craig be kicked out of the United States Senate.

Where was their outrage when Congressman Barney Frank Democrat from Massechusets, was running a whorehouse right out of his own house. Another Massechusets Congressman Democrat Gerry Studds was having sex with male pages. Did the Democrats demand that Studds resign for his deviant sexual behavior? Far from it, not only did Studds remain in office, he received a rounding applause upon returning to the house chamber after the scandal broke.

The truth of the matter is that Craig's real crime was that he is a republican, and liberals will take any opportunity to destroy the lives and careers of any republican.

I also thought that sexual matters were private and had nothing to do with a person being fit to hold national elected office. I guess having a young internal perform oral sex on you in the oval office is OK if you're Bill Clinton. Liberals can't say that the reason they were attacking Craig was that he was allegedly attempting to engage in gay sex. According to liberals like Hillary, conservatives are the homophobes that hate gays and liberals are the tolerant ones.

An Amoral Party

The truth is that democrats don't espouse any virtues at all. They support a culture of relativism where there are no standards of decency or right and wrong. Today's democrats are nearly totally amoral and devoid of any of the values that our country was founded on. Conservatives on the other hand do support traditional family values. Now, this isn't to say that conservative politicians lead lives devoid of sin. We are all sinners, and pray to God in our own ways to seek forgiveness. Being flawed, as all humans are, doesn't mean that we shouldn't try to support traditional family values and a sense of decency in our society.

Craig has been called a hypocrite upon the breaking of this scandal. Now, keep in mind that he plead guilty to a misdemeanor offense, and didn't actually perform deviant sexual acts like both Frank and Studds did. Craig also never sponsored a bill making it illegal to try and pick up a stranger in a public restroom to engage in gay sex. How exactly then is he a hypocrite? The answer is simple, he's a republican. Liberals will take any chance to ruin both the careers and lives of republicans.

Forcing Sex onto our Kids

Liberals will fight to allow sex education courses for kindergarteners. They want to take the words "One Nation under God" out of the pledge of allegiance and teach 5-year-olds how use condoms. A public school in Colorado put on mandatory assembly teaching students about all types of sexual acts including; man on man, woman on woman, and just for kicks they included man on woman.

For one thing, sexuality is a personal matter, especially when it comes to matter of homosexuality. For many, homosexuality is considered a deviant act. Now, this doesn't mean that anybody is talking about passing any kind of anti-gay legislation. However, we should be allowed to our own beliefs according to our own morals and religion. It is not the place of government to force the homosexual life style onto our children.

Liberals are so politically correct, that they won't even state that unprotected gay sex is one of the leading causes of spreading AIDS. Rather than potentially saving the lives of millions of homosexual men by having frank discussions about the dangers of unprotected gay sex, liberals like Hillary remain mute. Instead, they run campaigns on how AIDS is going to ravage through the straight community as well. During the Clinton administration, there was a government program to hand out free condoms to gays. It was discovered later than many of the condoms had holes in them. The administration didn't say anything, exposing the gays to the risk of contracting AIDS.

If a republican administration had kept something like this silent, the democrats would have accused them of attempted genocide of gay men. Liberals wont' even admit that the gay lifestyle does carry with it a higher risk of contracting the deadly disease. The truth is the AIDS is still mainly limited to gay men, and intravenous drug users. (Dope addicts that share dirty needles.)

Free Needles for Drug Users

In yet another stunning act, several liberal communities across the country have taken to handing out free needles to drug users. I personally don't want my tax dollars doing for clean needles for druggies. It's not that I want to see them get AIDS; it's that I do want to see laws enforced, and societies protected. Drug addicts commit crimes so that they can get the money they need to feed their addition. Taking illegal drugs in and of itself is also a crime. These people should be put in prison, and helped to kick their addiction if possible. However, giving a drug addict a needle is not helping anybody. I wonder if liberals like Hillary would ever agree to give a person addicted to tobacco free government cigarettes. How about creating a safe haven near Hyannis Port for addicts? What would Teddy think about dopers hanging out by the Kennedy Compound? I didn't use alcoholics as an example, for obvious reasons.

Deviance in the Arts

These people truly don't have their heads screwed on right. As Mayor of New York City, Rudy Giuliani was ridiculed for criticizing so called 'art' that included placing a crucifix in a jar of urine and a picture of The Virgin Mary covered in animal crap. Now, as a decent human being, you don't have to be Christian to know that those are truly offensive and in bad taste. Liberals were all espousing freedom of artistic expression. For one thing, there's a difference between art, and displays meant solely to offend. Mayor Giuliani wasn't trying to ban the displays; he just wanted to deny them any public funding. I agree, and don't feel that public monies should do to support those types of displays. In fact, I don't believe that tax dollars should be used for the arts. If there's a market for it, private galleries can display it. If the art is no good, it should remain obscure. I don't want bureaucrats deciding which art is good enough to spend our tax dollars on. I also don't believe that it is the role of government to fund those types of projects.

The same goes for public television. The government should immediately stop the funding of public television as well as NPR, National Public Radio. In the era of cable television, if a certain program that is currently on PBS is good, it will be picked up in a second. Do you really think that Sesame Street wouldn't survive if it weren't for the government? Of course it would, it would be picked up in a second if the PBS system was ever to be discontinued.

Liberals believe that they can't be held accountable for any of their own personal failings because they don't purport to have any virtues whatsoever. Back in the early 1990's there was the check bouncing scandal. Congressmen such as Dan Rostenkowski, Democrat from Illinois were writing checks that were bouncing left and right. There are actually two lessons to be learned from the check bouncing scandal. Liberals feel that they are so above the law, that writing hundreds of thousands of dollars in bad checks is nothing to them. Even after being convicted on felony counts Rostenkowski remained defiant.

Another lesson here is just how removed from reality politicians like Hillary Clinton really are. They've never had to live under the stupid laws that they pass for the rest of us, so they don't see the damage that they're doing. These guys weren't even competent enough to balance their own personal check books.

Former senator and 1972 Democratic presidential nominee George McGovern, who since leaving government has become the owner of a hotel in Connecticut, said that if he had had the experience of running a business before entering Congress, it would have changed his position on some issues. Welcome to reality Mr. McGovern, the laws you guys pass can be a pain in the ass for the rest of us.

Chapter #3

The Terrorist Candidate of Choice

Hillary will not enjoy a large degree of support from sectors of our society such as the military, veterans, the bible-belt, or members of the National Rifle Association. However, she will likely enjoy overwhelming support from members of CAIR – the Council on American-Islamic Relations. CAIR is a group that supports preferential treatment for Muslims living in this country, which in and of itself is only somewhat alarming.

What is truly disconcerting is their lack of vocal opposition to terrorist acts committed in the name of their religion. For one thing, CAIR does not want the United States to take an aggressive stance against Islamo-Fascism. I find this very alarming. If CAIR was really offended by the way Islamo-Fascists have corrupted their religion, where are the public displays of outrage? Their lack of any strong opposition to the atrocities committed by the Al-Qaeda types strips them of any real credibility. I thought that theirs was a religion of peace. Where's the outrage against the violence?!?

Bill Clinton frees 9/11 Hijacker

Mohamed Atta was one of the 9/11 hijackers who flew one of the planes into the Twin Towers on that faithful day in history. Now, was 9/11 preventable? If George H.W. Bush had been re-elected in 1992 it might have been. Certainly, Atta's role that day was totally preventable. The Israelis had Atta in prison for committing terrorist acts in their country. It was at the behest of Bill Clinton that the Israelis freed Atta. Atta showed his gratitude to America for securing his freedom from an Israeli prison by participating in the worst attack on our soil in our nation's history. Clinton's failures as Command-n-Chief are truly stunning, and there are people that are dead American's today because of it.

Arafat Love-Feast

How many of you know that Israelis cook their food with the blood of slaughtered Palestinian children? Well, that's the story at least from Suha Arafat, widow of the late Yasser Arafat. Hillary was present as a speech Mrs. Arafat was giving. Her speech was a baseless barrage of lies including accusations that Israelis murdered Palestinian women and children with poisonous gas. Through it all, Hillary just sat there nodding approvingly.

Now, had there been credible proof that the Israelis used poisonous gas against the Palestinians; there would of course have been an international outrage. OK, let me clarify, a legitimate international outrage. The outrage against Israel today are mostly from Arab nations that just plain hate Jews, and from other countries that lack the balls to stand up to the Arabs because of their oil.

After hearing Suha Arafat accuse Israelis of being nothing more than cannibals and mass murders, Hillary quickly gave her a nice big hug. Amazingly, Jews living in New York still supported this woman's candidacy for the Senate. I think that in all fairness, Hillary isn't necessarily anti-Semitic; she just doesn't give a damn about anybody but herself. She'd throw Bill under the bus if it was to her political advantage.

Bill Clinton also invited Arafat to the White House in 1993 to try broker a peace between Israel and the Palestinians. Now, in fairness to Clinton, he's not the first American President to make that mistake. What I do find stunning is that as usual the Jews were asked to make far more concessions than the Palestinians. It's usually something like, the Israelis give up a strategic part of their country to the Arabs, and the Arabs promise not to murder Jews. The Oslo Peace Accord which of course the Palestinians didn't abide by won Arafat the Nobel Prize for Peace. A known terrorist with the blood of thousands on his hands was awarded a peace prize. This is yet another stroke of liberal idiocy.

Now, Clinton and Carter being wrong when it comes to the Israeli-Palestinian conflict does not come as a surprise to me. I'm more surprised when they actually take a policy position that makes sense. Ask yourself, if the Palestinians stopped attacking Israel, would the Jews live and let live. The obvious answer is yes. Now consider the opposite.

Communists for Clinton

Cuban Dictator Fidel Castro has endorsed a Clinton – Obama ticket. Obviously the communist dictator can spot kindred spirits. He also knows that democrats like Hillary are more in line with Cuban's communist doctrine of total government control than the Republicans are. Hillary-Care is closely patterned after Fidel's and would have a similar impact on the United States as Castro's has had on the Cuban healthcare system. Amazingly, Michael Moore's latest film 'Sicko' holds up the Cuban healthcare system as something we should aspire to. Moore is just not the sharpest knife in the drawer. He is however very popular with the Clintons. During one of Bill's State of the Union speeches, Moore was sat right next to former President Carter. That's a place of honor if you're a liberal.

War on Terror

Another reason that Hillary has the Islamo-Fascist vote is that she would not be strong on the war on terror. Heck, liberals don't even want to use terms like 'war on terror' or 'Islamo-Fascists'. She's just another cut-n-run liberal that will take our brave troops out of Iraq before they've had a chance to complete their mission. For the good of our country, we can not afford to have to place another Clinton in the White House. For those who doubt me, let's take a quick look at the history of Bill Clinton's administration acts to combat terrorism.

The Sudan offered to turn Osama bin Laden over to Bill Clinton on several occasions. Clinton wanted no part of it, and turned them down each time. The head of Al-Qaeda could have been in United States custody back in the 1990's if not for the total dereliction of duty of Bill Clinton. During the numerous attacks on United States troops and civilians during the Clinton Administration, he took no military action. Whether it was the bombing of the World Trade Center back on 1993, the attack on the Khobar Towers, the attack on the USS Cole, and more, through it all Clinton remained mute. He was more interested in getting his next Lewinsky than in performing his Constitutional duties as Commander-n-Chief. In fact, if it weren't for Monica's grand jury appearance, Clinton would never have launched a missile attack against an aspirin factory in the Sudan.

Coddling the Terrorists

Many on the left have been very critical of what have been referred to as enhanced interrogation techniques. One such technique that gets a lot of press is water boarding, making a prisoner believe that they are going to drown. I will not come out and endorse torture. However, I personally have enough faith in our military that they know what lines they can and can not cross in the name of extracting information from captured terrorists. I also don't equate forcing terrorists to wear stockings and panties on their heads with the kind of medieval brutality the Islamo-Fascists practice.

Any American troops captured on the war on terror are mutilated and then killed. Those sick bastards even behead non-combatants such as journalist Daniel Pearl. Now, tell me why I should give a damn about water boarding, sleep deprivation, or slapping the shit out of a terrorist to uncover the next plot to kill innocent Americans.

President Hillary (*heaven forbid*) will likely grant the terrorists full access to the civilian courts as if they have been charged with crimes instead of committing acts of war against us. The few captured terrorists that have been released, have gone right back to the fighting, picking up arms against American troops. You don't release enemy combatants while the war is still being fought. If the war on terrorism lasts for 20 years, then I guess it sucks having to be a prisoner of war for that long, but they should have considered that before joining Al-Qaeda.

Anyway, far from torture, at Guantanamo, they get prayer rugs, darn good healthcare and culturally sensitive meals. If I were the warden there, those guys would have cement floors and be served nothing but pork, the other white meat. Pork chops, pork bologna, pork pudding, pork blood pie, pork ice-cream, puréed pork slushees. Well, I believe that I've made my point. Tongue and cheek aside, the Hillary's of the world should consider whether or not the terrorists would offer to give a captured American soldier that happened to be Jewish kosher meals to be culturally sensitive. The lesson here is stop coddling medieval bastards that want nothing more than to place the entire world under Sharia law. To them we are nothing more than infidels. Being a prison of war shouldn't be akin to staying at a Club Med. Most of the prisoners have it better living conditions at Gitmo than before they were captured.

Marines Out of Uniform

Hillary hates the military so much that as first lady, she insisted that Marines assigned to the White House not wear their military uniforms unless specifically required to as part of their duties. This woman actually banned our troops from wearing their uniforms. Hillary does not feel anything but loathing for our brave men and women that have volunteered to protect our freedoms. Do we really want a Commander-n-Chief that so hates her own troops that she doesn't even want to see them wearing the uniform? We all saw what a terrible Commander-n-Chief Bill Clinton the draft dodger was, do we really want to see how his wife would do?!? As a quick reminder, it was Jimmy Carter that pardoned all the draft dodgers, thus enabling Bill Clinton to run for the presidency.

Democrats are Dangerous

In all fairness to Hillary, the Islamo-Fascists would support any democrat candidate for president over a republican. Do you really think that bin Laden wants to see somebody like Rudy Giuliani in the White House? The dream-scenario for the terrorists in the general election would be Clinton running against Ron Paul. Bin Laden and other enemies that we face today know that they have a friend in the White House when a democrat is elected president. Perhaps the term friend isn't totally fair. A more accurate term would be a leader lacking the testicular fortitude to properly defend us against Islamo-Fascists. To put it another way, when it comes to fighting the war on terror, Hillary has no balls in more ways than one.

Beyond the failings of Bill Clinton that are listed above, consider the many failures of President Jimmy Carter. His failure to support the Shah of Iran thus allowing that country to become the anti-American extremist Islamic state that it is today. He followed up that stroke of international diplomatic genius by allowing the same Iranian radicals to hold U.S. citizens hostage for 444 days. It was truly stunning that a two-bit country with less military might than France had Carter cowering with indecision like a dear in the headlights for over a year. Beyond the tragedy of Americans being in captivity for that long was the fact that it showed our enemies that America was truly a paper tiger that lacked the guts to defend herself. If you doubt that our enemies fear a strong President, consider how long it took the Iranians to release the hostages once Reagan won the election in 1980. They were on a plane headed towards freedom before Reagan even took the oath of office. Reagan wasn't about to put up with that kind of foolishness, and the Iranians knew it. The 80's were a tough time for Arab terrorists. Carter wasn't satisfied with being one of the worst Presidents in modern history he wanted to keep doing harm to the United States even after he had left office. In 1994 this foreign policy guru helped to broker accords with North Korea. We would give them money, fuel and equipment, and they would promise not to build a nuclear weapon. Excuse the hell out of me but somebody please explain to me why we should allow a communist nut job like Kim Jong Ill to make those kind of demands on us? The leaders of these radical counties like North Korea and Iran never keep their promises. To them, they are just a ploy to buy more time. Even if one were to give a level credence to the good intentions of liberals, the fact is that aide given to dictators never actually makes it to the masses. In the case of North Korea, not only have they developed a nuclear bomb they are selling the technology to terrorist states such as Syria. Thanks again Bill and Jimmy.

People in countries such as North Korea and Iran are dirt poor while their leaders live like Kings. Liberals don't see the evil in men like Kim Jong Ill, Saddam Hussein, Osama bin Laden or Mahmoud Ahmadinejad. To Hillary types, the real evil in the world are conservatives. You don't see any rallies decrying the evil acts of Islamic terrorists, but you will see anti-Bush rallies. Liberals will greet Gorbachev with open arms, praising him as the great liberator of the Soviet Union. The truth is that the communist dictator couldn't stand toe to toe with Ronald Reagan, and his empire collapsed while trying. Reagan in a stroke of foreign policy genius freed all of Eastern Europe, hundreds of millions of people, from the horrors of Soviet oppression without firing shot. Of course while conservatives love The Gipper, according to Hillary, Bill was a much better president. I guess it would be a matter of "The Gipper' versus "The Zipper", or "The Great Communicator" versus "The Great Philanderer".

As a quick recap, Iran is an anti-American Islamo-Fascist nation thanks to Jimmy Carter. Osama bin Laden is the head of Al-Qaeda and not in a United States prison thanks to Bill Clinton. North Korea was allowed to become a nuclear power due to the efforts of both Carter and Clinton. The Islamo-Fascists gained in both strength and daring during the 1990's due to the inactions of Clinton. We are at war with Islamo-Fascists, and truly can not afford to have a democrat in the White House.

In times of peace, they just screw up the economy by raising taxes and out of control spending. The Carter economy was so bad that it was given the name stagflation. A period of high interest rates, high inflation and high unemployment. We are not at peace, despite the fact that liberals would like to tell you otherwise. When Clinton was claiming everything was rosy in the late 1990's think of Neville Chamberlain telling the British citizens the same thing in the late 1930's.

Chapter #4

A Sovereign Nation no More

The Illegal Immigration issue is quite possibly the most important domestic issue of our time. We are loosing our national identity due to an influx of people with no desire to become part of the American experience. Consider immigrants earlier in our nation's history, mostly from Europe. While maintaining a certain level of pride for their 'mother' country, they became Americans. They learned English and flew the flag of The United States. Many immigrants rushed to join the military to help defend their new country that they loved. My own ancestors came to the United States from Europe in the 1930's, and my father fought in World War II. Immigrants had to be sponsored by people living in America, and weren't not eligible for any social programs. My father would tell me stories of people living with them for a couple of months until they could afford their own place to live.

Contradict that with what we have now. Illegal immigrants today overwhelmingly have no desire to become Americans. Most consider themselves Mexicans living in the United States and not Mexican-Americans. Consider self-proclaimed immigration activist Elvira Arellano. She came into this country illegally several times in the 1990's and after being deported, came right back. She has given birth to a boy while living here illegally. She didn't bother getting married of course. Despite the fact that she has been here for over 10 years, she doesn't speak English. She has spent the last year living in the Adalberto United Methodist Church in Chicago where she enjoyed sanctuary. She took it upon herself to leave the church to speak at a pro-illegal immigration rally in Los Angeles. She was arrested and deported while at the rally. Now, once she arrived in Tijuana the Mexican government treated her has a celebrity.

If there was any doubt in anybody's mind that Mexico has absolutely no respect for our sovereignty, consider that Mexico has passed a law condemning her deportation and urging that she immediately be allowed to return to the United States. Amongst their reasons for urging that Arellano be allowed to return to the United States is so she can be reunited with her son, Saul. Bear in mind, the person responsible for Arellano being separated from her son is Arellano herself. She could easily arrange for her son to be with her in Mexico. It is unconscionable that a mother would leave her 8 year old child to live with strangers. If the Mexican government really cared about Saul and Arellano, they would fly the young boy to Mexico to reunite the child with his mother today.

Deporting Illegals Called Cruel

Deporting illegals has been called a hurtful cruel act because it often separates parents from their children. First of all, if as an American citizen I commit a crime and am sent to prison, aren't I separated from my family as well? Also bear in mind that when people make a conscience decision to come to the United States illegally and bring their families with them, they expose their children to certain risks. Furthermore, nothing is keeping illegals that have been deported from bringing their families with them back to Mexico.

The truth is that the Mexican government encourages illegal immigration of its citizens into the United States. Rather than try and fix any of the serious problems facing their country, they want to export them to us. Consider the informational pamphlets that the Mexican government hands out that to its citizens that actually tells them how to cross the border illegally. They are also condemning the plan to build a fence between the two countries. If they had any respect for our laws at all, we wouldn't have to build a fence to keep millions of their citizens from flooding into our country.

Mexican Immigration Policy

In an act of true hypocrisy, Mexico has very restrictive immigration laws. They only allow 3,000 legal immigrants into their country per year. Legal immigrants of Mexico are not eligible for any government social programs. Immigrants are not allowed to run for political office, and are forbidden from holding many government jobs. Try sneaking into Mexico illegally and see how friendly that government will treat you. The hypocrisy is like Michael Moore preaching to us about health care. Does the man even know what a salad bar looks like?

What do you think the Mexican government would do to you as an American if you were to get caught crossing into Mexico illegally with 700 pounds of marijuana? You'd probably be shot dead, and if not you'd certainly face years in a Mexican prison. I think that I'd rather be shot dead.

Our nation's stance on illegal immigration is so out of whack that when this really did happen here, the drug dealer was given amnesty to come into the United States any time he wanted. The only people doing time in prison are the two border patrol agents, Ramos and Compean. They shot the illegal immigrant drug dealer, who then ran back across the border. In an act of true liberal idiocy, the drug dealer was forgiven for any crimes he committed, and given a card allowing him to cross into the United States at any time. That is something that actually comes in handy as a Mexican drug runner.

Mohammad Garcia

Liberals liken enforcement of immigration law to harassing gardeners. To them, illegals are all law abiding people who want nothing more than to find a better life for themselves here in America. What they are too blind to see is that Islamo-Fascist terrorists are taking advantage of their ignorance on this issue as well. Many Arabs are having their names changed in Mexico in order to more easily pass for Mexicans. Our southern border is not just a port of entry for illegal immigration, it's also largely unguarded crossing for Arab terrorists as well. Since our government isn't making any real effort to find the illegals that currently live in this country, they also have no idea how many Islamic terrorists are currently living here that have crossed over from our unprotected southern border.

The Cost of Illegal Immigration

Liberals will state that we can't possibly deport the estimated 12 million illegals currently living in our country today. They say that it will cause an economic collapse. Wrap your mind around that concept for a moment. Deporting 12 million people, the majority of which don't even have a high-school education will destroy the strongest economy on the face of the planet. Liberals will also say how illegals are actually a financial benefit to our economy since they pay social security taxes but don't collect. For one, if Hillary had her way, I'm sure illegals would be eligible to collect social security. Secondly, illegals are a multi-billion dollar drain on the economy.

Illegals come into our country, and the good hearted liberals immediately give them free healthcare (check out emergency room), food stamps, public education for their children and more. In many cases, illegals are given in-state tuition discounts at public universities. As American citizens we're forced to establish residency in the state the university is located in order to be eligible for in-state tuition. As an illegal, you just have to not get deported long enough, and you're eligible. To a liberal, the American citizen is second class behind the illegal alien. If you're a conservative, perhaps not even that. Economists often state that money rarely leaves the economy. We earn our wages, and spend it to purchase goods and services. Many illegals send the wages that they earn back to Mexico. It's a multi-billion dollar benefit to the Mexican economy. In many grocery stores in the south-western United States, you'll see illegals purchasing groceries with food stamps, and then wire their cash back to their families in Mexico.

Many illegals will use hospital emergency rooms as their primary care providers. By law, hospitals can't refuse to provide service based on an inability to pay. Many hospitals have actually opted to close their emergency rooms rather than to try and absorb the hundreds of millions of dollar of losses that they would have to incur by treating illegals for free. Interestingly enough, Mexico has a law that pays for the healthcare costs of their citizens anywhere in the world. Do you think as president that Hillary will try and get Mexico to reimburse the United States for the billions in health care costs that their citizens have racked up over the years? I wouldn't hold my breath if I were you.

Illegal Alien Criminals

It is also estimated that one-quarter of our prison population is comprised of illegal aliens. Now, don't get me wrong, we have our own share of American citizens that are bad dudes and commit heinous crimes as well. However, when somebody is arrested for a crime, there's a federal requirement that efforts must be made to determine if they are in this country legally. If they are in fact illegal, the federal authorities (ICE) are to be notified. There are municipalities across the country that are violating this government mandate. Sanctuary cities they are often called.

In August of 2007 three young people were brutally murdered in an execution style killing. One of the suspects in this truly heinous crime was an illegal alien named Jose Carranza. The fact that Carranza is an illegal alien isn't in and of itself telling. The real tragedy is that he has a felony rap sheet a mile long, and the local authorities failed to notify ICE and have this guy deported. You hear stories all the time about local authorities not reporting to ICE when they have arrested illegals. How many people have to be murdered, raped or killed by drunk drivers before liberals feel that somebody is not adding to the fabric of our society?

Liberal will state that you can't turn an illegal into ICE just for being arrested because they haven't been convicted of anything yet. To do so would be a violation of the Constitutional guarantee of innocent until proven guilty. The truth is that they aren't being turned into ICE for the crime(s) that the locality has arrested them for. They are being turned over to ICE for being in the country illegally. Also bear in mind that the most solemn duty of our government is to protect the citizenry. By not protecting us the illegal aliens, the government is being derelict in this matter.

Through it all, where does Hillary stand? She is a pro-amnesty liberal. To hell with the impact that the tens of millions of illegals are having in this country, there's a huge voting block there. Remember, with Hillary it's all about her. As President, do you really think that Hillary will see that the fence on our border with Mexico will be completed? Never mind that a law was passed in 2006 to have the fence built. As of late 2007 less than 20 miles of fence have been completed. That's something like one mile per month.

Do you really believe for a second that she would encourage ICE to aggressively enforce American immigration laws? She would grant legal status if not full citizenship to the estimated 12 – 20 million illegals currently living in this country. I can guarantee you that President Hillary will not pass a law denying any federal monies from municipalities that don't enforce immigration laws? She's also not going to be high on the idea of fining businesses that knowingly hire illegal?

Ingles Solamente (English Only)

Do you think as the president that Hillary would fight to make English the official language? Don't get me wrong, I have nothing against people that speak two or more languages. In fact, I have a certain amount of respect for people that can converse in numerous languages. However, to paraphrase Teddy Roosevelt, this country has room for one language and one flag. You don't see government documents written in; German, Italian, Greek, French or any of the other dozens of languages that are spoken by immigrants in this country. The obvious reason is that they all know English as well. If Mexican-Americans want to be able to speak Spanish in addition to English, more power to them. However, we shouldn't give preferential treatment to one segment of society because they refuse to join the great American experience. Perhaps we should remind liberals that printing government documents in both English and Spanish uses more paper and requires more energy. That might actually get their attention.

The interesting thing is that the sector of the society that is impacted the greatest by illegal immigration are the young and the poor. Low skilled, entry level jobs are being taken over by illegals. English only speakers are being turned away from certain jobs because the illegals only speak Spanish. Try getting a job as a cook or a dishwasher in the fast food industry in Arizona or southern California if you don't speak any Spanish. The unemployment rate amongst the most vulnerable sectors of our society is higher as a direct result of illegal immigration.

Joe Arpaio is the Sheriff of Maricopa Country in Arizona. He is a very outspoken sheriff who has taken a strong stance against illegal immigration. Arpaio has setup a telephone hotline where people can call in if they suspect that somebody is in this country illegally. The sheriff's department will conduct an investigation, and only take action if there is *probable cause* to believe that a law has been broken, including being in this country illegally.

Now, as you can imagine, the liberals are having a fit about this. They are saying that having this type of hotline is unconstitutional. What I find even more interesting is the fact that Arizona also has a hotline to report illegal smoking. Now, liberals love that hotline. Apparently, according to liberals, second hand smoke is more dangerous that millions of people living in our country illegally. The last time I checked people don't commit identity theft in order to purchase a pack of cigarettes. Teen-agers with fake ID's maybe, but not full scale ID theft like illegals are guilty of. However, illegals routinely commit crimes such as identity theft, providing false documentation and perjury.

You won't hear Hillary condemning illegals for breaking our immigration laws, or committing ID theft or perjury. To her, they're just about of hard working people just trying to get a better life for themselves and their families. At the risk of sounding cold hearted, we can't be the social welfare state for the world. There are hundreds of millions of people living in far worse poverty than those in Mexico. We can't import the poor of the world and have them live off of the social programs that liberals like Hillary love so much. For a liberal, the real dilemma would be what to do if they were to catch an illegal that was smoking a cigarette.

Illegals Perform the Work American Won't

Another often used yet bogus argument of the left is that illegals are doing that work that Americans won't do. I personally find it insulting that liberals insinuate that Americans are lazy and afraid of hard work. Now, the types of jobs that illegals hold aren't limited to picking fruit from the fields either. Go to airports in California and Arizona, and most of the workers are Mexicans. Now, go to the airports in the north-eastern parts of the countries and you'll see both whites and blacks working there.

Elvira Arellano, the illegal 'activist' that was hiding out in a church for over a year had herself worked in an airport. The question one has to ask is just how thorough are the background checks of airport employees in a post 9/11 world if an illegal can get a job at an airport?

Now I will say that there is a job that most Americans just won't do, and is something that is better suited to illegal aliens. I am referring of course to the 6 men that planned on attacking Fort Dix. Attacking a military installation on United States soil is a job most American citizens just won't do. Hillary, I guess you got me on that one.

Remove the Incentives

Most illegals that do come here do so for jobs. Even jobs paying $6 - $10/hr are far better than almost anything they could ever get in Mexico. So, if the government would pass laws that punish businesses that hire illegals, the jobs would go away and so would most of them. Most illegals would self-deport if they found themselves out of work, and were denied access to any social programs.

The federal government should assess stiff fines and penalties for businesses that knowingly hirer illegal aliens. Egregious offenders should lose their business licenses. Let a few McDonalds restaurants get closed up for loosing their business licenses and the rest will get the message. Now in fairness, the government needs to provide a system to allow employers to easily check the accuracy of the documents that job applicants produce when applying for work. Similar to the instant background check that is in place to check on people who want to purchase firearms. Of course to a liberal, a law abiding citizen owning a gun is more of a risk than an illegal alien.

No More Anchor Babies

It was never the intent of the 14th amendment to the Constitution to grant citizenship status to the children of aliens living in this country illegally. Besides, in Lincoln's time, there wasn't the huge illegal immigrant problem that we are facing today. The fact is that to change the anchor baby issue doesn't even require amending the Constitution. Simple legislative action could clear up that inappropriate application of the 14th amendment.

Deportation for Life

If you come into this country illegally, and are deported, you should be barred from ever legally immigrating for the rest of your life. With that kind of risk hanging over their heads, many illegals would probably self-deport and attempt to enter legally, rather than risk permanent deportation.

Sanctuary Cities

Many cities across the country have openly defied federal law by refusing to take any actions against illegals. When illegals are arrested they don't notify ICE as is required by law. Many illegals that have committed numerous serious felonies are allowed to roam free on the street to prey on unsuspecting citizens. The federal government should deny municipalities any federal funding if they openly defy the laws in this matter. Mayors that have taken an oath to uphold the law should be subject to recall and removal from office for breaking the law. Better yet, throw a few of the mayors in jail for openly defying federal law, and watch the rest fall in line.

Our Economy Is Dependent on Illegals

Liberals love to say how our economy would be ruined if all the illegals immigrants currently living in this country were to be deported. Now, I will admit that a sudden exodus of 12 – 20 million people would have a tremendous impact on several facets of our economy. There would be a flood of houses for sale on the market, and that is something that we don't need right now. The current housing market is not in the best of shape. Fast food chains across the south would be scrambling to hire teen-agers again. Limousine liberals like Hillary Clinton and Nancy Pelosi would be frantic to find people to mow their lawns. Businesses would have to hire from a labor pool of American citizens and legal temporary workers. They may even have to raise wages in certain areas.

However, our economy would survive. If we can survive four years of the Carter administration, our economy can withstand anything. The truth is that we would realize a massive reduction in cost in areas such as welfare, food stamps and healthcare. Class room sizes would go down and more. There would be a net gain in the area of hundreds of millions, if not billions, of dollars to off set the losses that such a mass exodus would create.

Wrong is Wrong

I also submit that being dependent on an illegal or immoral labor source does not justify its existence. This is a lesson that southern democrats like Hillary haven't learned through our Nation's history. You see, illegals from Mexico aren't the first controversial labor source that democrats have been in favor of. Today it is illegal aliens, back in the 1800's it was slavery. Having a cheap source of labor that is illegal and/or immoral is not right. It wasn't then, and it isn't now. I'm sure the economy of the south was impacted when the slaves were freed. It didn't mean that freeing them was wrong. Slavery is one of the darkest times in our Nation's history. Wrong is wrong, and democrats like Hillary are constantly on the wrong side of these types of issues.

It goes without saying that blacks are far better off in this country today than their ancestors were under the bonds of slavery. The same holds true for illegals. Those that want to follow the law and come into this country legally will ultimately be far better off than they are today. Living with the fear of deportation and being afraid to contact the police if you're a victim of crime is no way to live. To fully and openly participate in the American experience you must be here legally. Illegals come here for a better life, but if they would actually come here legally, they would enjoy the full richness that our country has to offer.

Chapter #5

Hillary-Care

Shortly after taking office in 1993 Bill Clinton established the Task Force on National Health Care. He put his wife Hillary in charge of the project and she was to come up with a 'comprehensive' plan to provide universal health care for all Americans (legal or not). In a speech that Bill made to Congress in September 1993, he stated that following:

"Millions of Americans are just a pink slip away from losing their health insurance, and one serious illness away from losing all their savings. Millions more are locked into the jobs they have now just because they or someone in their family has once been sick and they have what is called the preexisting condition. And on any given day, over 37 million Americans -- most of them working people and their little children -- have no health insurance at all. And in spite of all this, our medical bills are growing at over twice the rate of inflation, and the United States spends over a third more of its income on health care than any other nation on Earth."

For a first lady to be placed in charge of national policy making was unprecedented. It is speculated that Bill put her in that role as a quid pro quo for her standing by his side during his numerous extramarital affairs, and even defending him against the evil vast 'right-wing' conspiracy.

Now even though the United States has never had a totally socialized health care system, it does have publicly funded health care programs for the elderly, the disabled and the poor with programs such as Medicare and Medicaid. Current federal law, that did exist back then, guarantees public access to emergency room services regardless of the ability to pay. So, the notion that Americans don't have access to health care is just wrong, and pandering to the emotions of liberals. We not only provide health care for the poor that are in this country legally, we provide the best healthcare in the world for illegals as well. Visit the emergency room of a hospital that is located in Arizona. You'll see illegals using them as their primary health care provider. Yet another cost that as citizens we are being asked to absorb. I'm sure the prisoners at Guantanamo Bay have better healthcare, as prisoners of the United States than they did as members of either the Taliban or Al-Qaeda living in some middle-eastern hell hole like Iran.

Aspects of Hillary-Care included having the Government deciding which doctors that we as Americans would be allowed to see. It would have made it a criminal offense if we decided to see another doctor, even if we paid for the visit ourselves. Yep, you could be jailed for the offense of going to a doctor of your own choosing. The federal government would hand out allotments of money to the different areas of the country to cover the costs of health care for the year. Of course, nobody had a real good answer for what would happen if 7 months into the year, certain areas ran out of funds. Would people that were living in areas with no more money for health care have to do without? Would they have to travel to other areas that still had money? Of course that would result those in other areas using up their government allotted health care budget quicker. The reality is that the government would have to provide additional monies, which of course would result in cost over runs. That is not at all unusual for any government entitlement program. Overages as much as 5 to 10 times cost estimates are common. The Clinton-Gore recession of 200 would have been a full blown economic meltdown had Hillary-Care become the law of the land. What truly makes me sick (pun intended) is that if elected, we'll see Hillary-Care Act II in 2009. Quick – where's my barf bag. Please don't tell me I'll have to go to Mexico to seek healthcare.

Hillary-Care would have socialized a full 1/7 of the entire economy of the United States. A plan that was so extreme even democrats voted it down. Then New York Senator Daniel Patrick Moynihan stated that there was no health care crisis in the country, but more of an insurance crisis. A man that was by no means a right winger also stated that *"anyone who thinks [the Clinton health care plan] can work in the real world as presently written isn't living in it."*

What I find most astounding is that the evidence that Hillary-Care would have been a total disaster for the country can be seen all around us. Socialized medicine has failed in each and every country that is has ever been tried in. Canadians have such a long wait for critical health care procedures that many are dying while waiting to see a doctor. Canadians that have the financial resources often travel here to the United States seeking treatment. The old joke back when Hillary-Care was being dreamed up was that if it passed, the Canadians would have no place to go for their medical care. Every country that has socialized medicine has waiting lines for life saving procedures that are months long. France has socialized healthcare, and coincidently enough some of the highest tax rates as well. They have a statistic that boasts how the French have the best healthcare in the world, as evidenced by the fact of the great longevity. First of all, the French being overly high on themselves is nothing new. Secondly, in all fairness, the French generally do have a diet that consists of less fat that we do here in America. Of course, not having to deploy troops in a time of war, even when the enemy is on your own soil also helps skew those good ole' longevity numbers as well.

Chapter #6

Bring on the Tax Hikes

One of my biggest criticisms of the Bush administration is that he wasn't conservative enough. For a full six years his party had a majority of both houses of Congress. When the republicans lost in 2006, it was mainly due to conservatives getting frustrated. Where was social security reform, why aren't we protecting our borders especially in a time of war, why aren't we drilling for oil in ANWR in an effort to lessen our dependency on foreign oil?

One of the biggest mistakes that Republicans make, and President Bush in particular, is trying to be civil and cooperate with democrats. In doing so, they miss out on passing meaning legislation that the country desperately needed. When the movie '13 Days In October' first came out, Bush invited Senator Ted Kennedy for a viewing with the him in the White House. After all, both John and Bobby were central figures in that drama back in 1962. For the president's noble act of reaching across the isle,

Kennedy hasn't exactly been very kind to him. The truth is that republicans often try and take the high road and deal civilly with democrats, who in turn are playing ruthless gutter politics.

Even with a majority in both houses of Congress, Bush still compromised on his tax cuts by allowing dates to be set for them to expire. Many will do so in 2010. Now, democrats have a majority in both houses, and if Hillary wins in 2008, you can bet your paycheck that the Bush tax cuts will fade away into history. That will by no means be the first tax increase that we as Americans would see in a Hillary administration.

One of Hillary's first acts as president will most likely be to pass tax increases that will make what Bill did in 1993 look like the ante in a nickel and dime poker game. As stated in chapter 5, that woman wants universal healthcare coverage for all Americans, well liberals at least. Hillary-Care along with every kind of government entitlement program the extreme left can dream up will require money. Liberals don't equate lower taxes with increased revenues in to the treasury. This despite the fact that it happened under the administrations of both John Kennedy and Ronald Reagan when they lowered taxes. It's also happening today as a result of Bush's tax cuts. A country trying to attain greater economic prosperity by raising taxes is like a man standing in a bucket and trying to lift himself up by the handle.

Higher taxes will result in an economic slow down, as was witnessed during the failed administration of Jimmy Carter. The government will actually see less monies coming into the treasury as a result of the economic slowdown brought on by the higher taxes. At that point, being the good liberals that she is, Hillary will either raise taxes even higher, or have the federal government spend more money going deeper into debt, or most likely a combination of both.

For those considering voting for Hillary, none of which would be reading this book, just imagine that vote costing you hundreds of dollars each and every paycheck. The reality is that it will.

While I was sitting in a political science class in the early nineties, I addressed the class full of liberals with a way to ensure that 100% of all tax dollars collected for the poor would go directly to help those in need. Every two weeks, when you take your paycheck to the bank to get cashed, a welfare recipient will be there waiting for you. You give that person a couple of hundred dollars, or whatever you feel is fair, or for a liberal, what the welfare recipient says is fair. They all looked at me as if I were nuts. Why would they want to give a total stranger hundreds of dollars out of each and every paycheck that they work hard to earn? Of course, my response to them was to ask what exactly did they think that government handouts were. At least with my plan, all of the money would go directly to the poor without upwards to 40% being used spent on bloated ineffective government bureaucracies.

Most people really have no idea how much of their earnings gets confiscated by the government in the form of one tax or another. Even today, most American work until May to pay the taxes to the government at all levels. If Hillary becomes our next president, be prepared to work until sometime in June to cover taxes, before you earn a dime for yourself. Just a quick reminder, ours is a free-market system based on capitalism right?

Chapter #7

Energy Policy

(Lack Thereof)

America is far too dependent on foreign oil. That is one statement that I believe both liberals and conservatives can agree upon. However, the agreement stops there, because why we are dependent and ways to ease that dependence vary greatly from the left to the right.

Energy Independence

I am a huge believer in American ingenuity, and believe that as a nation we can solve any problem when we put our minds to it. Making up less than 5% of the world's population we've invented most of the new gadgets and gismos that exist today. I mean come on, do you really think France was going to invent the personal computer or Iran the cell phone! A lot of the comforts that are taken for granted today by people around the world would not exist if not for the inventive energies right here in America. If I sound like I love this country, you're damn right I do.

Just as we've conquered other problems in our Nation's history, we can conquer our dependence on foreign oil as well. We can take some meaningful steps right now, without having to invent the car that runs on water. We need to start drilling for oil in ANWAR and other places that have large deposits of that black gold. Hillary and other lefty loonies in the Senate pat themselves on the back for defeating the effort to open ANWAR to oil drilling during Bush's first term. They said that it would ruin its natural beauty and harm wildlife. Again, Hillary is playing to the lunatic fringe, in this case environmentalist wackos.

ANWAR is so remote that the only humans that would ever see the oil rigs would be the oil workers themselves. It's also a myth that wildlife is harmed by pipelines and oil rigs. The wildlife living near that Alaskan pipeline actually like it. It provides warmth, and it is not uncommon to see animals near the pipeline to stay warm. I guess global warming hasn't quite reached Alaska yet.

American oil companies also lost a bid to drill off the coast of Florida. Again, thanks to liberals and environmentalist extremists. Cuba is drilling there, and of course their safeguards are far superior to those of American oil companies. Kind of the same way that according to Michael Moore, the

Cuban healthcare system is better than ours as well.

America also has one of the largest deposits of sweet coal in the world. Of course we can get at it because of Bill Clinton. He declared the entire area a reserve so that no coal removal would be permissible.

Not only do we have a bad energy policy, we have a refining capacity issue as well. Thanks to lunatic environmentalists, there hasn't been an oil refinery built in this country since the 1970's. The amount of regulations and fees that are involved make it economically impractical to build an oil refinery. Our population has increase by over 50 million people since the 70's, and yet we haven't increased our refining capacity one iota.

Just Do with Less

Hillary's answer to energy independence is for Americans to just do with less. Turn in the SUVs and big Trucks, and drive little two-door 4 cylinder jobs. Now, I'm all for conserving where possible, but these people want to take us back to the 1900's. I'm also not against taking public mass transit where possible. However, in some cities it's just not practical. For example, Arizona just doesn't have a mass transit system that is comparable to the BART (**B**ay **A**rea **R**apid **T**ransit) system in California. Furthermore, not too many people are going to want to wait at a bus stop in Phoenix Arizona in the summer when it's over 100 degrees.

It also sounds somewhat hypocritical for liberals to say that we should just get by with less, as they jet around the country in private airplanes. I doubt you'll ever see Hillary flying coach. Come to think of it, I don't think there's an airsick back that's big enough to serve most conservatives if we were forced to sit by that woman for a cross-country flight. When liberals say things like '*there's just too much consuming going on*', they of course mean that we should cut back so they can live their extravagant lifestyles.

APEC

The Arab oil producing nations have an organization called OPEC, which stands for the Organization of Petroleum Exporting Countries. Oil that costs them approximately one to two dollars a barrel to extract from the earth, they turnaround and charge $80/barrel or more. Now, in a true free market system, they can charge all they want. However, most OPEC nations are countries whose governments are hostile to America and to the west in general. It also is not good foreign policy to purchase billions of dollars in oil from countries that support terrorist acts against us.

Aside from seeking out domestic sources of energy as previously discussed, western nations should also consider forming APEC or the Agricultural Producing Exporting Countries. If OPEC wants to charge $80/barrel for oil, we can charge them equally inflated prices for food. The truth is that if it weren't for their oil, the middle-eastern Arab nations would wither and die. Most don't have any industry to speak of outside of their oil, and don't produce near enough agriculture to feed their people. We can drill for oil domestically and find alternative forms of energy easier than they can grow food in the desert.

Chapter #8

The Un-Patriotic Left

Liberals of today are not the same as they were 40 or 50 years ago. Do you think we're ever hear Hillary give a speech telling the American people to *'Ask not what your country can do for you, ask what you can do for your country.'* Those immortal words were spoken at the 1961 inaugural speech by President John F. Kennedy. Say what you will, but he certainly was not a member of the 'vast right-wing conspiracy'. A sense of duty and service were alive and well in those days, and it crossed party lines. Being in the military didn't necessarily mean you were a republican as there was actually a pretty good split between the two major political parties. Today, the vast majority of men and women serving in our military are republicans because quite frankly most democrats hate the military, and certainly don't believe that America is worth fighting for.

Hollywood Decay

Moral termites must have been eating away at the decency of Hollywood types for decades. The likes of John Wayne, Audie Murphy and

Jimmy Stewart have been replaced with; Sean Penn, Michael Moore, Rosie O'Donnell, Tim Robbins, Brian de Palma, Jane Fonda and more. While in the name of political correctness, most have been resistant to challenge the patriotism of extreme leftist, I don't have that particular weakness. I personally believe that political correctness is hurting this country by not challenging the indefensible actions of liberal extremists.

Making my top 10 list of American traitors is movie producer Brian de Palma. He has recently released a film called 'Redacted'. In it he portrays the American soldiers fighting the war on terror as a butch of animals raping Iraqi women. Now, the hard truth is that atrocities happen in all wars. I'm sure that there were instances of inappropriate actions in every war that our country has fought since the revolution itself. They don't say war is hell for nothing.

In those extremely rare instances where an American soldier does act inappropriately they face quick and severe penalties. The Uniform Code of Military Justice is much stricter than civilian laws. I will also state that as a veteran, that there is no more honorable group of people than the members of the United States military. They put their lives on the line to protect our freedoms. You sure as hell don't join the military to for the fantastic salary. Consider films of the 20th Century that was often incredibly patriotic. I'm not just referring only to films about the Korean Conflict and World War II; even movies about Vietnam painted our soldiers in a very popular light. This was despite the fact that Vietnam itself was very controversial. It will be a cold day in hell before I watch a Brian de Palma film ever again.

Tim Robbins recently said that American soldiers have killed 400,000 Iraqi civilians. So, not only are liberals like Robbins un-patriotic they aren't very bright either. Even according to liberal sources, nowhere near that many Iraqi civilians have lost their lives since the start of the American invasion. The figure is likely closer to around 80,000, most of which have been killed by insurgents and not by American troops. Robbins should open his eyes and realize that we've freed the Iraqi's from the horrors of Saddam Hussein. We aren't even fighting the Iraqi government over there anymore. Hussein is dead and buried, and now we're actually fighting Iranian troops, Al-Qaeda and other terrorist forces. America is just as much liberating Iraq today as we freed France from Nazi occupation back in the 1940's.

Michael Moore, the man who could act as a stunt double for Fat

Bastard from the Austin Powers movies is another un-patriotic intellectual lightweight. His two recent movies are yet more examples of Hollywood leftists having taken the off-ramp on the informational super-highway. You have Fahrenheit 911 making wild accusations and being very critical of the Bush administration's actions in the wake of the September 11th terrorist attacks. I'm sure Bill Clinton would have had a better plan. It would most likely have consisted of a visiting Monica and trying not to stain another one of her dresses. Perhaps she should have worn a rain slicker when servicing Clinton, this way he could have wiped off his semen before she left of Oval Office.

Moore's other movie 'Sicko' actually takes the position that Cuba's healthcare system is better than ours. Just how far removed from reality does somebody have to go before democrats or the drive-by media challenges them. Does anybody with an I.Q. higher than room temperature really believe that the healthcare system of Castro's Cuba is better than what we have here in the United States? It's interesting, but when world figures and the extraordinarily rich from around the world are truly sick, they will often come to the United States to seek out the best medical care on the planet. How many Arab princes have rushed to Cuba for treatment upon being diagnosed with cancer?

Rosie O'Donnell spent her one year on the television show the View lambasting Bush, our troops and the country as a whole. One of her accusations consisted of saying how our government had tortured 9/11 mastermind Khalid Sheik Mohammed since capturing him back in 1993. She even showed a picture of the poor mistreated terrorist. Here again, is yet another example of a liberal getting their facts wrong. Mohammed wasn't captured until 2003, so she's off by a decade. The photo that she used to show what a decade of torture can do to a man was taken before he was even in American custody. This guy just looks like crap naturally. Kind of the same way that Rosie does. She also stated that we shouldn't be condemning Islamo-Fascists without criticizing Christian-Fascists. Again, this is yet another glaring example of a Hollywood elitist that has taken a serious detour off the intellectual super-highway. Christian's don't behead non-Christians. Christianity is truly a religion of peace and tolerance. Nowhere in the bible does it state that you should murder non-believers, or seek martyrdom so you can be rewarded in the after-life with 72 virgins.

Sean Penn is actually more stupid than dangerous like the other ones. His star is not as bright any more, so he's not able to do as much damage. You'll remember that he's the intellectual lightweight that went to Iraq while the country was still ruled by Saddam Hussein to see for himself if he was indeed a dictator.

Of course Saddam didn't show Penn the rape rooms, the torture chambers, or the wood choppers that he used to feed his own countrymen into. I also doubt that Penn was given a tour of the mass graves that Hussein had or shown the truck loads of chemical and biological weapons that were being shipped out of Iraq in advance of the impending American invasion. Penn did get to see a number of ornate Presidential palaces, and a bunch of hand-picked loyalists saying how much they loved their benevolent leader. Gullibility thy name is liberal.

Jane Fonda, a name so synonymous with being a traitor that nothing more needs to be said.

Even entertainment executives are letting their left wing tendencies effect their business decisions. Disney is refusing to release the movie, 'The

Path to 9/11' out of DVD. The movie is critical of the Clinton administration, and Hillary is running for President. Now, in all fairness, it might not be a matter of liberalism as much as self-preservation. People with dirt on the Clintons often find themselves taking a permanent dirt nap. Just what kind of telephone conversation did a member of the Clinton crowd have with Disney?

If you doubt the criminal nature of the Clinton machine, consider that Kathleen Willey's house was broken into. You'll remember Kathleen Willey, she went to see Bill Clinton at the White House the day her husband committed suicide. She was hoping he would help her out in light of her recently family tragedy. Bill being the total scumbag that he is took the opportunity to make un-welcomed sexual advanced towards Willey. The N.O.W. crowd again had to lower the bar so not to be critical of their man Bill Clinton. They said that it's OK to grope a woman once, but if she says no, you can't do it again. That must be good news for perverts everywhere. Well, liberal perverts anyway.

Well, her house was recently broken into. The only thing that the burglars stole was a copy of her manuscript. No money, jewels, nothing of value except the manuscript. You see, Hillary needs to know if there's anything in there that might harm her presidential campaign. Breaking and entering is not a crime if you're a Democrat. I guess Nixon's biggest crime was being a Republican in Public.

Un-Patriotic Elected Officials

One could excuse to a certain degree Hollywood liberals that are totally removed from reality from becoming extremists, but it is completely inexcusable from our elected officials. I say this because lunatic Hollywood types like Michael Moore don't get to vote on Iraq funding bills. However, Hillary voted to deny our troops that are in harms way needed funding. She also voted to force a timeline for withdrawal. That's retreat and surrender in plain English. Those are not the traits of somebody that's qualified to be our next president. Harry Reid has proclaimed to the world that the war is lost. Ted Kennedy said that Abu Ghraib was still open for business, just under new management. The champion of Chappaquiddick was insinuating that our government was just as bad as Hussein's government. Chuck Shumer, democrat Senator from New York, declared that the reductions in violence in Al-Umbar Province were not a result of the hard work of American troops and the surge, but despite their incompetence. He credited all the progress to the local War Lords. Between Chuck Shumer and Hillary Clinton, I can't say that there's a lot of depth of patriotism from the senators from New York.

Senator Dick 'Turbin' Durbin, democrat from Illinois has accused our troops of Nazi-like behavior. He has said that atrocities committed by American soldiers in Iraq, were *"not isolated incidents but crimes committed on a day-to-day basis with the full awareness of officers at all levels of command"*. Between Durbin, and the freshmen Senator who believes that he's qualified to be the President, Illinois doesn't have a strong Senatorial team. This is a steep decline from the state that gave us Abraham Lincoln.

Dennis Kucinich, Democrat Congressman from Ohio and presidential candidate actually criticized America at a time of war in an interview while in Lebanon. This mental midget praised Syria, a terrorist nation for taking in 1.5 million Iraqi refuges. He also blasted the Bush administration for it 'illegal' occupation of Iraq. Ask yourself, what would have happened to an elected official had they gone to Italy, criticizing Franklin Roosevelt and praising Japan and Germany in 1943. Does this sound like a man with the depth of seriousness to be Commander-n-Chief?

To bring up John F. Kennedy again, in his day it was said that if you wanted to be elected to public office, you'd better be a veteran. That's how patriotic the country was in the years after World War II and Korea. It wasn't a liberal thing or a conservative thing, it was just that as a whole the country realized the value of having worn our Nation's uniform. Today, if you openly support the troops, the liberals tar you as a right wing extremist. If that's their litmus test, then consider me a right wing extremist.

Liberals Vested in America's Defeat

Amazing as it sounds, today's liberal democrat party have tied their political fortunes with the terrorists. Many have said that any victories in Iraq will hurt their electoral prospects in 2008. Stunning as it may seem, is the fact that today's liberal democrat party is hoping that Islamo-Fascists kill as many of our troops as possible. They believe that dead American soldiers will translate into more votes for them. One of their biggest fears is the report on the surge given by General David Petraeus. Despite obvious signs that the surge is having a positive effect, the liberals have dismissed any signs of progress in Iraq. Again, what is good for America is deemed back for democrats. Considering the progress that has been made as reported by General Petraeus on September 10th, consider what may be possible throughout the end of 2007 and into 2008. That is something that has democrats quaking in fear. They know full well that if things in Iraq keep improving that they will likely face defeat in the 2008 elections. Again, what's good for America is bad for the democrats.

Franklin Delano Roosevelt was the president during all but the last few months of World War II. You never heard republicans rooting for either the Germans or the Japanese in hopes that it would help their electoral prospects. What do you call it when your words and actions provide aide and comfort to the enemy in a time or war? The answer is treason. Many of today's liberal democrats have certainly crossed the line of being unpatriotic, while others have committed acts that could be considered treasonous.

MoveOn.Org

Lunatic leftist organizations such as MoveOn.Org and the Daily Kos have all the rights in the world to be as extreme as possible. A glaring example of their extremism was on display on early September 2007. Just days prior to the report that General Petraeus delivered to Congress in the progress of the surge in Iraq, MoveOn.Org took out a full-page newspaper ad calling him General "Betray Us". Now, America is a free country, and I wouldn't support our government censoring this kind of garbage even though I do find it reprehensible. What I find even worse is that there are no democrats criticizing MoveOn.Org for it. In fact, just the opposite, Hillary has taken tons of cash from them, and the party leadership holds regular conference calls with them. The democrats are so beholden to the wacko left in this country that they truly are "A National Party No More" to quote Zell Miller.

For that matter, outside of conservative talk radio, and the Fox News Channel, where is the mainstream media that considerer themselves journalists and not liberal hacks? I guess the real question is just how far does a somebody have to the left be before a liberal will say that a line has been crossed?

Liberal Mindset: Dead Soldier Good - Dead Civilians Bad

While liberals like Hillary are hoping for terrorist victors in Iraq, they fear an attack between now and the November 2008 election here on United States soil. Liberals like Hillary believe that can freely criticize the Bush administration's handling of the war in Iraq. Their willing accomplices in the liberal press will down play any progress and focus on every IED that goes off from now until the election. However, they know that they can't stand toe to toe conservatives when it comes to responding to the immediate aftermath of an attack on our soil.

Somehow candidates like; Giuliani, Thompson, Romney and McCain are more convincing when talking about an appropriate American response to a terrorist attack than Hillary. Hell, Senator B. **Hussein** Obama's answer to what he would do after a terrorist attack on our soil, when we knew who attacked us was to deploy FEMA. That's even weaker than President Bill Clinton's responding to numerous acts of terrorism that were committed against America during his administration. You'll remember that his response was to have the FBI investigate them as if they were criminal acts instead of acts of war. Here's a clue for today's liberal democrats; the best federal agency to seek out for an appropriate response to a terrorist attack on our soil is not DHS or DOJ but the DOD.

A Pro-Western Arab Democracy in the Middle-East

Iraq is an important front in the overall war on terror for several reasons. From strictly a humanitarian perspective, freeing millions of people from the horrors of a maniacal dictator is a good thing to do. Liberals should applaud the fact that Iraqi women are no long being violated in government run rape rooms, or that the Bathists are no longer putting Iraqi citizens into wood chippers. Hussein was also harboring terrorists, and had held numerous high level meetings with Al-Qaeda. Let's not forget that under Hussein's rule, the Iraqi government wrote checks for $25,000 rewarding the families of suicide bombers that had blown themselves up while murdering innocent Israeli civilians.

Removing Saddam from power changed Iraq from being a safe haven for Al-Qaeda, to a central front on the war on terror. The enemy knows that a stable pro-western democracy in the heart of the middle-east is a very dangerous thing for their cause. It is also better for America to fight the war on terror on foreign soil than in our own towns and cities. If Hillary becomes the president in January 2009, she'll bring our troops currently serving in Iraq home. Of course, the terrorists will come here as well. With all of the mistakes that the Bush administration has made in Iraq, it is important to bear in mind that there hasn't been a terrorist attack on our soil in September 11, 2001. In fact, with of the criticisms, the government has actually thwarted numerous attacks.

The Pro-Terrorist Rights Party

Hillary and her liberal ilk have bemoaned many aspects of the Patriot Act. An act that the liberals actually supported in the immediate aftermath of 9/11. Yet another liberal flip flop. One of the most glaring examples of liberal lies that harmed America's efforts to fight the war was their attacks against wire tapping. First of all, it was unconscionable that they would reveal this classified effort during a time of war. Secondly, they lied to the American people by saying that the government was eavesdropping on the telephone conversations of Americans happening entirely on U.S. soil. The truth is that the wire tapping program was listening in on conversations where one of the parties was located outside of the United States.

Conservatives understand the value to intercepting the conversations that potential terrorists that are already on American soil are having with their overseas counterparts. Simply being located on American soil shouldn't mean that a suspected terrorist should be free of any government surveillance. They even went as far as revealing some of the surveillance techniques, allowing our enemy to adapt.

The Clinton administration was in fact eavesdropping on Americans. Project Echelon as it was called, was capable of scrutinizing just about every fax, e-mail, phone call and telex message in the world. And like every other system during the Clinton years, especially the two desperate years preceding the election of 1996, it was fully capable of being abused. It doesn't take a huge leap of faith to believe that the administration that was involved in Filegate would have used Echelon to spy on their political opponents. Remember, to a republican, terrorists are the enemy, but to Bill and Hillary Clinton, republicans are the enemy.

Chapter #9

The Clinton Legacy

It is important to understand the power of the Presidency. The effects a president can have on America and the world often extend far beyond their time in the White House. Let's look at some of the legacy of Bill Clinton's 8 years as president.

A Stronger Al-Qaeda

As I have stated earlier, the most wanted many on the planet could have been in United States custody today if not for the incompetence of Bill Clinton. The Sudan had offered to hand over the leader of Al-Qaeda over to the Clinton administration on not less than three occasions. Each time, our then Commend-n-Chief turned them down. Through the numerous attacks against the United States during Clinton's two terms he failed to act appropriately.

On 26 February 1993, a car loaded with 1,200 pounds of explosives blew up in a parking garage under the World Trade Center, killing six people and injuring about a thousand others. The blast did not, as its planners intended, bring down the towers. Four followers of the Egyptian cleric Sheik Omar Abdel Rahman were captured and convicted of the World Trade Center bombing in March 1994, and sentenced to 240 years in prison each. The purported mastermind of the plot, Ramzi Ahmed Yousef, was captured in 1995, convicted of the bombing in November 1997, and also sentenced to 240 years in prison. Harsh prison sentences for certain, but an inappropriate response to an act of war.

On 13 November 1995, a bomb was set off in a van parked in front of an American-run military training center in the Saudi Arabian capital of Riyadh, killing five Americans and two Indians. Saudi Arabian authorities arrested four Saudi nationals whom they claim confessed to the bombings, but U.S. officials were denied permission to see or question the suspects before they were convicted and beheaded in May 1996.

On 25 June 1996, a booby-trapped truck loaded with 5,000 pounds of explosives was exploded outside the Khobar Towers apartment complex which housed United States military personnel in Dhahran, Saudi Arabia, killing nineteen Americans and wounding about three hundred others. Once again, the U.S. investigation was hampered by the refusal of Saudi officials to allow the FBI to question suspects.

On 7 August 1998, powerful car bombs exploded minutes apart outside the United States embassies in Nairobi, Kenya, and Dar es Salaam, Tanzania, killing 224 people and wounding about 5,000 others. Four participants with ties to Osama bin Laden were captured, convicted in United States federal court, and sentenced to life in prison without parole in October 2001.

On 12 October 2000, two suicide bombers detonated an explosives-laden skiff next to the USS Cole while it was refueling in Aden, Yemen, blasting a hole in the ship that killed 17 sailors and injured 37 others. No suspects have yet been arrested or indicted. The investigation has been hampered by the refusal of Yemeni officials to allow FBI agents access to Yemeni nationals and other suspects in custody in Yemen. Armed attacks against our military are not to be treated as civilian criminal acts, but as acts of war.

You'll notice through the chronology that the attacks get more brazen. That's to be expected as each time Clinton failed to respond appropriately, the enemy got more emboldened. Clinton's dereliction of duty culminated in Al-Qaeda launching the most deadly attack on U.S. foil for a foreign enemy in our country's history on September 11, 2001.

When the Clintons moved from Arkansas to Washington D.C., they brought their pattern of corruption with them. At least for 8 years it was safe to purchase land in Arkansas again.

Travel-Gate

Within first months of taking office, Clinton fired the entire Travel Office staff. Admittedly, while harsh on the employees themselves, not one that would have a huge impact on the country as a whole. What was stunning, and showed just how ruthless Bill and Hillary are, is that they sicked the FBI on Billy Dale, the Travel Office Director at the time. It demonstrated that the Clintons were willing to use the full resources of the United States Government to personally attack anybody they saw as a political threat.

File-Gate

Clinton, without any warrants or probable cause, searched the FBI files of more than 700 republicans. He was obviously looking for any dirt that he could use against them. That deafening silence that you heard during that particular scandal was the ACLU not saying a damn thing in protest about the civil liberties of republicans being violated. When this one hit the fan, they blamed the entire affair on Craig Livingstone. He was in charge of personnel security at the White House at the time. While testifying under oath he swore that he couldn't even remember who offered him the position. Trust me; if somebody offers you a job at the White House, you're going to remember their name. So for a liberal to English translation, Livingstone was lying under oath, aka perjury.

When is 8 Greater Than 93

Attorney General Alberto Gonzalez eventually resigned under the fall out for over the firing of 8 federal prosecutors. Democrats, Hillary included were accusing of Bush administration of partisan firings for dismissing the 8 prosecutors. Now, flash back to 1993, and Bill Clinton fired all 93 federal prosecutors during his first year in office. He didn't even have enough time to review their records to claim that the firings were justifiable. He wanted them out, and his liberal cronies in.

An ACLU Lawyer on the Supreme Court

Ruth Bader Ginsburg, a justice on the Supreme Court was a Clinton appointee. Now, a sitting President has the power to appoint justices that are then subject to Senatorial approval. Before being nominated to the highest court in the land, Ginsburg was a lawyer for the ACLU. Clinton didn't pick a centrist, and even a serious Constitutional scholar for such a high post, but a radical leftist. As of 2007, she's still on the Court, and continually takes a liberal stance on issues brought to the bench with no regard for the Constitution. If Hillary is elected on 2008, we can look forward to more extreme lefties to be nominated to the bench.

Zipper-Gate

I won't rehash Clinton's scandal with Monica Lewinsky here again. I can even to some extent buy into the notion that a person's private life is private, and not all personal failings means that you're not fit to hold office. What I do find stunning is that the entire affair went far beyond oral sex. Clinton lied to the American people, he lied under oath and through it all the left supported him. If it appears today that our country is more divided now than ever, consider that the left has sold their souls to the Clintons.

In any sense of intellectual honesty, Bill Clinton would be shunned by society. A man that disgraced his office; dishonored his wife, harmed his daughter and lied to the very American people that he took a oath to serve, should fade away into obscurity. Instead, Clinton writes books, delivers speeches, and is actively helping Hillary with her Presidential campaign. A man that you can't trust to be alone with their 17 year old daughter is not somebody to be admired.

Clinton's Women

Bill Clinton is more than a man with a healthy libido, he's a sexual predator. He had affairs with Monica Lewinsky and Gennifer Flowers. He made unwelcomed sexual advances towards Kathleen Willey and Paula Jones. The scandal with Ms. Jones was where in typical leftists attack mode James Carville called her trailer trash. Since the left had sold their soul to the Clintons, women's groups such as NOW stood by their man Billy through it all. Even a credible accusation of rape as is the case with Juanita Broderick doesn't raise any concern for liberals. I can guarantee you that if George Bush slapped a woman on the ass that the Nation Organization of Women would be screaming for his resignation. Hell, Senator Larry Craig was forced to resign from the Senate for doing a lot less than what Clinton did. Headlines for Craig should read "Cruising While Conservative". For those that believe that minorities are targeted by racism, consider that the current under-class in this country is the conservative.

Illegal Campaign Cash

For any of you that think a Hillary presidency will be any less of a disaster for America than Bill's was, consider that the exact same pattern of corruption under Bill is continuing with her. In the 1990's Clinton took illegal campaign money from John Huang. In payment, Huang was given access to national security secrets, which he in turn gave to China. Today, Hillary was caught taking illegal campaign money from Norman Hsu. The Chinese must know that they can get more national security secrets if Hillary is elected president.

A Chinese Base on American Soil

Under the Clinton administration, the military base in Long Beach California is now under lease to the Chinese Ocean Shipping Company. For those of you on the left, China is a communist country, so the Chinese Ocean Shipping Company is run by the government. The deal went through with no input by the National Security Council or the Central Intelligence Agency. Does it come as a surprise that illegal arms shipments into the

United States have been traced back to the Chinese run shipping port? I wonder how much money John Huang had to bride Clinton with to persuade him to turn a base on Long Beach over the communist China.

Free Government Housing for a Multi-Millionaire Former President

Former presidents get Secret Service protection for life, and rightfully so. The Clintons, being class acts are actually charging the Secret Service to be housed in quarters that are on the same property as their home in New York. The fee that the Clintons are charging is equal to the monthly mortgage on the entire property. Yep you got, the government is paying the Clinton mortgage. That's just what this country needs, welfare for millionaires. I suppose Bill and Hillary are going to apply for food stamps next.

Corruption the Arkansas Years

Even before 1993, the Clintons were a perfect team for being as corrupt as you could possibly be. Hillary made $100,000 on one deal in cattle futures. When a futures analyst was asked how something like that was possible, the answer is it isn't, well at least not legally. They also screwed over hundreds of Arkansas residents in their Whitewater scandals while at the Rose Law firm. Now, liberals will say that of course the Clintons are innocent because they were never proven guilty in a court of law. There's a fine line between being innocent, and practicing a pattern of cover-ups and corruption that thwart the prosecutorial process. During Star's investigation, evidence that had been subpoenaed was withheld. Billing records magically turned up two years later in the private residence of the White House. Translation, Hillary had them hid under her bed.

Some of the principle players that were involved in the White Water scandal in addition to Bill and Hillary included such notable figures as; Webb Hubbell and James and Susan McDougal. Neither Webb nor the McDougal's were willing to testify during the investigation. In fact, Susan McDougal spent time in prison rather than cooperate. That's either real friendship or real fear. Either way, not only should you not let the Clinton's baby sit your daughter, don't want to buy land from them either. There's the risk of getting screwed in both scenarios.

When Bill campaigned in 1992 promising the most ethical administration in history, conservatives knew that he was full of shit. Like I have said before, liberalism is an emotional ideology. The left is emotionally tied to the Clintons, so they excuse anything that Bill and Hillary do. Conservatism is an intellectually based ideology, and for the most part takes an honest look at the facts. For instance, you didn't see conservatives backing the 1997 amnesty for illegal immigrants bill just because George Bush supported it. We stand by our principles, and are more tied to issues than to personalities. John McCain seriously harmed his presidential aspirations, by cosponsoring the amnesty bill with Ted Kennedy. Republicans aren't going to blindly support McCain because he's a republican. Contradict that with Hillary who can be both pro-war and anti-war and enjoy support from the same group of people.

Cash for Pardons

The Clintons will do anything and I mean anything to further them selves politically and personally. Nothing is too low or too harmful to our country for the team of Bill and Hillary. Consider that Bill pardoned hundreds of convicted felons during his presidency. In fact, over 140 **people** were pardoned on the last day of his presidency. Perhaps I should change the word **people**, to **campaign contributors**. He must have gotten one hell of a paycheck from that. Now, while legally there is nothing that can be done to reverse a presidential pardon, where's the outrage. If not for Fox News and conservative talk radio, that entire incident wouldn't have gotten any attention at all. Of course, when George Bush commuted the sentence of Scooter Libby, the mainstream press was all over that, screaming corruption. The total lack of any intellectual honesty on the behalf of liberals is stunning. Hell, even Hillary herself was accusing Bush of improprieties for the Libby commutation. The wife of the man that sold well over 200 pardons during his time in the White House has no business opening her mouth about this. As former White House Press Secretary Tony Snow asked, what's the Arkansas word for Chutzpah?

Summary

The pattern of corruption of Bill and Hillary spans decades and is truly stunning. What is stunning is not that there are corrupt people living in America today. The stunning part is that two of the most corrupt people are a former President and a sitting Senator who's running for president. Is there any illegal or immoral act that Bill or Hillary could do that would cause the left to sit back and take notice? I've come to a point where I seriously doubt it. Sexual Affairs – Perjury – Dereliction of Duty – Rape – Lying to the American People – Illegal Business Dealings – and through it all the Clintons are the darlings of the American left.

I believe that she's a shoe-in (or perhaps Hsu-in) to win the nomination in the primaries. The test for her will be that she has to stand toe to toe and debate whoever wins the republican candidacy. Hillary hasn't had to answer tough questions anytime during her entire adult life. As a liberal, she has been coddled by the media and has never had to stand on her own two feet. The best hope for America is to watch her crash and burn as she tries to debate a Romney, a Thompson or a Giuliani during the general election. I actually like Newt Gingrich's idea of a series of 90-minute debates between the candidates that is not moderated. Let the presidential hopefuls have these types of meaningful debate versus the 60-second sound bite format. Let the American people get a full taste of what a Hillary presidency would mean to this country.

Haven Help Us

Appendix A

Date	Contributor	Amount ($)	Recipient
05/10/04	Norman Hsu	2000	DNC
07/08/04	Winkle Paw	1000	John Kerry
07/19/04	Marina Paw	350	John Kerry
07/21/04	Norman Hsu	2000	John Kerry
07/27/04	Alice Paw	250	John Kerry
07/27/04	Bill Nelson Paw	500	John Kerry
07/27/04	Dimple Paw	250	John Kerry
07/27/04	Alice Paw	250	John Kerry
07/28/04	Winkle Paw	1000	John Kerry
08/06/04	Norman Hsu	2000	John Kerry
09/27/04	Peter Tan	3000	DNC
09/27/04	Danny Lee	1000	DNC
09/27/04	Danny Lee	1250	DNC
09/30/04	Norman Hsu	500	Barbara Boxer
09/30/04	Norman Hsu	2000	Barbara Boxer
09/30/04	Norman Hsu	12000	DSCC
10/05/04	Danny Lee	500	Tom Gallagher
10/05/04	Marina Paw	500	Tom Gallagher
10/11/04	Danny Lee	1000	DNC
10/12/04	Norman Hsu	5000	Florida party
10/13/04	Danny Lee	1500	DSCC
10/19/04	Norman Hsu	2000	Barack Obama
10/22/04	Norman Hsu	10000	Wisconsin party
10/25/04	Danny Lee	1000	DSCC
10/25/04	Danny Lee	1500	Ted Kennedy
10/25/04	Norman Hsu	2000	Ted Kennedy
10/25/04	Norman Hsu	2000	Ted Kennedy
11/01/04	Danny Lee	500	DNC
11/01/04	Norman Hsu	2000	Doris Matsui
12/23/04	Winkle Paw	2000	Hillary Clinton

Date	Contributor	Amount	Recipient
12/23/04	Winkle Paw	2000	Hillary Clinton
12/23/04	Norman Hsu	2000	Hillary Clinton
12/23/04	Norman Hsu	2000	Hillary Clinton
02/02/05	Norman Hsu	2000	Barbara Boxer PAC
02/03/05	Norman Hsu	5000	Obama PAC
02/04/05	Norman Hsu	2000	Doris Matsui
02/04/05	Norman Hsu	2000	Doris Matsui
02/13/05	Danny Lee	1900	Ted Kennedy
02/13/05	Marina Paw	2000	Ted Kennedy
02/13/05	Winkle Paw	2100	Ted Kennedy
02/13/05	Winkle Paw	1900	Ted Kennedy
02/23/05	Su Paul	300	Doris Matsui
02/23/05	Danny Lee	2100	Doris Matsui
02/25/05	Marina Paw	250	Doris Matsui
02/25/05	Winkle Paw	250	Doris Matsui
03/16/05	Marina Paw	1900	Hillary Clinton
03/16/05	Marina Paw	2100	Hillary Clinton
03/17/05	Winkle Paw	2100	Hillary Clinton
03/18/05	Danny Lee	2500	Obama PAC
03/18/05	Marina Paw	1500	Obama PAC
03/18/05	Winkle Paw	5000	Obama PAC
03/21/05	Su Paul	1000	Hillary Clinton
03/21/05	Danny Lee	500	HILLPAC
03/21/05	Marina Paw	500	HILLPAC
03/21/05	Winkle Paw	500	HILLPAC
03/22/05	Su Paul	500	Ted Kennedy
03/23/05	Yu Fen Huang	500	Maria Cantwell
03/27/05	Danny Lee	2100	Hillary Clinton
03/27/05	Danny Lee	2100	Hillary Clinton
03/31/05	Norman Hsu	5000	HILLPAC
03/31/05	Norman Hsu	2100	Debbie Stabenow
03/31/05	Norman Hsu	2100	Debbie Stabenow
05/13/05	Su Paul	2500	Obama PAC
05/13/05	Winkle Paw	2100	Debbie Stabenow
05/13/05	Winkle Paw	2100	Debbie Stabenow

Date	Name	Amount	Recipient
05/17/05	Norman Hsu	2100	Maria Cantwell
05/17/05	Norman Hsu	2100	Maria Cantwell
05/25/05	Norman Hsu	5000	DNC
05/26/05	Danny Lee	1000	Harold Ford
06/06/05	Norman Hsu	2100	Harold Ford
06/06/05	Norman Hsu	2100	Harold Ford
06/07/05	Danny Lee	2100	Patrick Kennedy
06/07/05	Danny Lee	2100	Patrick Kennedy
06/07/05	Marina Paw	300	Patrick Kennedy
06/07/05	Winkle Paw	500	Patrick Kennedy
06/07/05	Norman Hsu	2100	Patrick Kennedy
06/07/05	Norman Hsu	2100	Patrick Kennedy
06/09/05	Su Paul	4000	DSCC
06/09/05	Danny Lee	5000	DSCC
06/09/05	Winkle Paw	5000	DSCC
06/09/05	Norman Hsu	26700	DSCC
06/10/05	Su Paul	900	Hillary Clinton
06/10/05	Marina Paw	200	Hillary Clinton
06/21/05	Marina Paw	500	Debbie Stabenow
06/28/05	Marina Paw	500	Doris Matsui
06/28/05	Winkle Paw	500	Doris Matsui
06/28/05	Norman Hsu	2100	Doris Matsui
06/30/05	Norman Hsu	5000	DNC
07/13/05	Norman Hsu	2100	Bob Casey
07/13/05	Norman Hsu	2100	Bob Casey
08/23/05	Norman Hsu	1000	EMILY
08/31/05	Su Paul	1500	Debbie Stabenow
08/31/05	Marina Paw	400	Debbie Stabenow
08/31/05	Marina Paw	1600	Debbie Stabenow
09/12/05	Su Paul	2000	Harold Ford
09/14/05	Winkle Paw	250	Harold Ford
09/15/05	Su Paul	600	Debbie Stabenow
09/15/05	Su Paul	1400	Debbie Stabenow
09/23/05	Lelawattie Su	2000	Maria Cantwell

Date	Name	Amount	Recipient
09/23/05	Su Paul	2000	Maria Cantwell
09/23/05	Yu Fen Huang	1500	Maria Cantwell
09/24/05	Danny Lee	1000	Frank Pallone
09/24/05	Danny Lee	1000	Frank Pallone
09/24/05	Danny Lee	1000	Frank Pallone
09/24/05	Winkle Paw	1000	Frank Pallone
09/24/05	Winkle Paw	1000	Frank Pallone
09/26/05	Yu Fen Huang	2000	Patrick Kennedy
09/26/05	Marina Paw	500	Patrick Kennedy
09/26/05	Winkle Paw	1400	Patrick Kennedy
09/26/05	Winkle Paw	1600	Patrick Kennedy
09/30/05	Winkle Paw	1000	Joe Biden
09/30/05	Winkle Paw	750	Maria Cantwell
10/15/05	Vivian Paw	2100	Hillary Clinton
10/15/05	Stanley Lim	500	Hillary Clinton
10/15/05	Bill Nelson Paw	1000	Hillary Clinton
10/15/05	William Paw	1000	Hillary Clinton
10/15/05	Yu Fen Huang	2100	Hillary Clinton
10/15/05	Yu Fen Huang	2100	Hillary Clinton
10/24/05	Su Paul	600	Ted Kennedy
10/24/05	Su Paul	1600	Ted Kennedy
10/24/05	Danny Lee	200	Ted Kennedy
10/24/05	Marina Paw	2100	Hillary Clinton
10/25/05	Marina Paw	1000	DSCC
10/25/05	Winkle Paw	2500	DSCC
11/02/05	Su Paul	2000	Claire McCaskill
11/02/05	Danny Lee	400	Claire McCaskill
11/02/05	Danny Lee	2100	Claire McCaskill
11/28/05	Su Paul	1500	Joe Biden
11/28/05	Winkle Paw	900	Joe Biden
11/28/05	Winkle Paw	1100	Joe Biden
12/07/05	Su Paul	250	Nicholas Lampson
12/07/05	Danny Lee	650	Nicholas Lampson
12/07/05	Danny Lee	2100	Nicholas Lampson
12/07/05	Winkle Paw	300	Nicholas Lampson
12/08/05	Su Paul	1000	Harold Ford

Date	Name	Amount	Recipient
12/08/05	Yu Fen Huang	2100	Harold Ford
12/08/05	Danny Lee	1000	Harold Ford
12/08/05	Marina Paw	1000	Harold Ford
12/08/05	Winkle Paw	1000	Harold Ford
12/13/05	Danny Lee	600	Ted Kennedy
12/13/05	Winkle Paw	1000	Nicholas Lampson
12/14/05	Lelawattie Su	2100	Hillary Clinton
12/14/05	Lelawattie Su	2100	Hillary Clinton
12/14/05	Soe Lee	750	Hillary Clinton
12/14/05	Soe Lee	1400	Hillary Clinton
12/14/05	Soe Lee	2100	Hillary Clinton
12/16/05	Su Paul	1000	Bill Nelson
12/16/05	Danny Lee	400	Bill Nelson
12/16/05	Danny Lee	2100	Bill Nelson
12/16/05	Norman Hsu	500	Bill Nelson
12/16/05	Norman Hsu	2100	Bill Nelson
12/19/05	Su Paul	666	Debbie Stabenow
12/19/05	Su Paul	666	Dianne Feinstein
12/19/05	Soe Lee	666	Debbie Stabenow
12/19/05	Soe Lee	666	Dianne Feinstein
12/19/05	Yu Fen Huang	666	Debbie Stabenow
12/19/05	Yu Fen Huang	666	Dianne Feinstein
12/19/05	Yu Fen Huang	900	Harold Ford
12/19/05	Winkle Paw	1000	Maria Cantwell
12/23/05	Danny Lee	900	Doris Matsui
12/30/05	Su Paul	566	Maria Cantwell
12/30/05	Su Paul	1000	Maria Cantwell
12/30/05	Soe Lee	666	Maria Cantwell
12/30/05	Yu Fen Huang	666	Maria Cantwell
01/13/06	Danny Lee	1000	Kirsten Gillibrand
01/28/06	Peter Tan	2100	Hillary Clinton
01/28/06	Peter Tan	2100	Hillary Clinton
01/28/06	Stanley Lim	2000	Hillary Clinton
01/28/06	Bill Nelson Paw	1100	Hillary Clinton
01/28/06	Bill Nelson Paw	2100	Hillary Clinton

Date	Name	Amount	Recipient
01/28/06	William Paw	2100	Hillary Clinton
01/28/06	William Paw	2100	Hillary Clinton
02/10/06	Danny Lee	2000	Dianne Feinstein
02/21/06	Danny Lee	250	Bob Casey
02/27/06	Soe Lee	1066	Debbie Stabenow
02/27/06	Soe Lee	1433	Debbie Stabenow
02/27/06	Yu Fen Huang	1066	Debbie Stabenow
02/27/06	Yu Fen Huang	1433	Debbie Stabenow
02/27/06	Danny Lee	5000	HILLPAC
02/28/06	Su Paul	2500	Obama PAC
02/28/06	Soe Lee	5000	Obama PAC
02/28/06	Yu Fen Huang	2500	Obama PAC
02/28/06	Yu Fen Huang	2500	Obama PAC
03/02/06	Su Paul	1100	Dianne Feinstein
03/02/06	Su Paul	1400	Dianne Feinstein
03/07/06	Yu Fen Huang	1000	John Carter
03/07/06	Danny Lee	1000	Scott Kleeb
03/09/06	Su Paul	500	Bob Casey
03/10/06	Marina Paw	1000	Harold Ford
03/10/06	Winkle Paw	850	Harold Ford
03/11/06	Soe Lee	2000	Harold Ford
03/12/06	Danny Lee	500	Bob Casey
03/13/06	Su Paul	1000	Tammy Duckworth
03/14/06	Yu Fen Huang	500	Tammy Duckworth
03/14/06	Marina Paw	2300	Hillary Clinton
03/14/06	Marina Paw	2300	Hillary Clinton
03/14/06	Winkle Paw	500	Tammy Duckworth
03/16/06	Marina Paw	700	Debbie Stabenow
03/21/06	Soe Lee	400	Claire McCaskill
03/21/06	Soe Lee	2100	Claire McCaskill
03/21/06	Yu Fen Huang	2100	Claire McCaskill
03/21/06	Marina Paw	2000	Claire McCaskill

Date	Name	Amount	Recipient
03/21/06	Winkle Paw	2500	DSCC
03/21/06	Winkle Paw	1000	Claire McCaskill
03/21/06	Soe Lee	1000	White House
03/23/06	Marina Paw	500	Debbie Stabenow
03/28/06	Su Paul	1000	Scott Kleeb
03/28/06	Soe Lee	5000	HILLPAC
03/29/06	Su Paul	2000	DSCC
03/29/06	Yu Fen Huang	2500	DSCC
03/29/06	Danny Lee	2000	DSCC
03/29/06	Marina Paw	2500	DSCC
03/30/06	Su Paul	500	Tyson Pratcher
03/30/06	Su Paul	2000	Debbie Stabenow
03/30/06	Soe Lee	3000	DSCC
03/30/06	Danny Lee	250	Tyson Pratcher
03/30/06	Marina Paw	500	Tyson Pratcher
03/30/06	Winkle Paw	250	Tyson Pratcher
03/31/06	Su Paul	500	EMILY
03/31/06	Su Paul	-1966	Debbie Stabenow
03/31/06	Su Paul	400	Claire McCaskill
03/31/06	Soe Lee	1433	Dianne Feinstein
03/31/06	Soe Lee	2066	Dianne Feinstein
03/31/06	Yu Fen Huang	1433	Dianne Feinstein
03/31/06	Yu Fen Huang	2066	Dianne Feinstein
03/31/06	Marina Paw	1000	Dianne Feinstein
03/31/06	Winkle Paw	1000	Dianne Feinstein
03/31/06	Winkle Paw	500	Obama PAC
04/18/06	Danny Lee	2000	DNC
04/18/06	Marina Paw	2500	DNC
04/21/06	Winkle Paw	2000	DNC
05/10/06	Lelawattie Su	2000	Debbie Stabenow
05/12/06	Su Paul	250	Steve Filson
05/12/06	Danny Lee	250	Steve Filson
05/21/06	Su Paul	200	Bill Nelson
05/22/06	Su Paul	200	Claire McCaskill
05/22/06	Su Paul	200	Maria Cantwell
05/25/06	Danny Lee	1000	Robert

Date	Name	Amount	Recipient
			Menendez
05/26/06	Yu Fen Huang	500	Patrick Murphy
06/05/06	Yu Fen Huang	-566	Maria Cantwell
06/08/06	Vivian Paw	1000	Claire McCaskill
06/08/06	Soe Lee	500	Claire McCaskill
06/08/06	Yu Fen Huang	500	Claire McCaskill
06/08/06	Danny Lee	500	Claire McCaskill
06/08/06	Marina Paw	400	Claire McCaskill
06/08/06	Winkle Paw	500	Claire McCaskill
06/25/06	Alice Paw	1900	Hillary Clinton
06/25/06	Alice Paw	2100	Hillary Clinton
06/26/06	Yu Fen Huang	400	Patrick Kennedy
06/30/06	Su Paul	5000	DSCC
06/30/06	Soe Lee	3500	DSCC
06/30/06	Marina Paw	500	Kirsten Gillibrand
06/30/06	Winkle Paw	250	Kirsten Gillibrand
07/01/06	Normal Hsu	1000	Dianne Feinstein
07/14/06	Danny Lee	2500	DNC
07/17/06	Vivian Paw	1000	Jon Tester
07/18/06	Soe Lee	750	Jon Tester
07/18/06	Soe Lee	2000	Bob Casey
07/18/06	Yu Fen Huang	500	Jon Tester
07/18/06	Yu Fen Huang	500	Bob Casey
08/07/06	Normal Hsu	10000	Tennessee party
08/15/06	Bill Nelson Paw	1500	Claire McCaskill
08/22/06	Marina Paw	250	Jim Webb
08/23/06	Vivian Paw	500	Jim Webb
08/23/06	William Paw	500	Jim Webb
08/23/06	Soe Lee	750	Jim Webb
08/23/06	Soe Lee	1000	Tammy Duckworth
08/23/06	Yu Fen Huang	500	Jim Webb
09/09/06	Bill Nelson Paw	500	Jim Webb
09/11/06	Dimple Paw	500	Harold Ford
09/14/06	Su Paul	250	Jim Webb
09/14/06	Normal Hsu	10000	New York party
09/18/06	Bill Nelson Paw	1000	Jon Tester
09/18/06	Dimple Paw	1000	Jon Tester

09/18/06	Su Paul	250	Jon Tester
09/18/06	Danny Lee	250	Jon Tester
09/19/06	Su Paul	500	DSCC
09/19/06	Soe Lee	500	Daniel Akaka
09/19/06	Yu Fen Huang	500	Daniel Akaka
09/19/06	Yu Fen Huang	2000	DSCC
09/19/06	Danny Lee	2000	DSCC
09/19/06	Danny Lee	250	Jim Webb
09/19/06	Marina Paw	250	Tammy Duckworth
09/19/06	Winkle Paw	250	Tammy Duckworth
09/20/06	Dimple Paw	500	Jim Webb
09/21/06	Bill Nelson Paw	500	Harold Ford
09/21/06	Bill Nelson Paw	500	White House
09/21/06	Dimple Paw	500	White House
09/23/06	Bill Nelson Paw	500	Kirsten Gillibrand
09/23/06	Dimple Paw	500	Kirsten Gillibrand
09/23/06	Su Paul	250	Kirsten Gillibrand
09/28/06	Normal Hsu	10000	Tennessee party
09/29/06	Dimple Paw	2000	Claire McCaskill
09/29/06	Vivian Paw	500	Claire McCaskill
09/29/06	Winkle Paw	500	Claire McCaskill
09/30/06	Winkle Paw	-250	Tyson Pratcher
10/12/06	Su Paul	1000	DNC
10/13/06	Su Paul	2000	Bob Casey
10/13/06	Soe Lee	2000	Pennsylvania party
10/13/06	Yu Fen Huang	1000	Bob Casey
10/14/06	Danny Lee	1000	Hillary Clinton
10/14/06	Winkle Paw	1000	Hillary Clinton
10/14/06	Winkle Paw	1000	Hillary Clinton
10/14/06	Danny Lee	1000	Hillary Clinton
10/16/06	Su Paul	2000	DNC
10/16/06	Winkle Paw	1000	DNC
10/25/06	Stanley Lim	500	Harold Ford
10/25/06	Stanley Lim	2100	Hillary Clinton

Date	Name	Amount	Recipient
10/25/06	William Paw	500	Harold Ford
10/25/06	Vivian Paw	500	Harold Ford
10/31/06	Stanley Lim	500	Sherrod Brown
10/31/06	Stanley Lim	500	Tammy Duckworth
10/31/06	William Paw	500	Tammy Duckworth
10/31/06	William Paw	500	Sherrod Brown
10/31/06	Su Paul	500	Tammy Duckworth
10/31/06	Yu Fen Huang	500	Tammy Duckworth
10/31/06	Vivian Paw	500	Sherrod Brown
10/31/06	Vivian Paw	500	Tammy Duckworth
11/03/06	Norman Hsu	10500	Harold Ford
11/17/06	Su Paul	5000	Joe Biden PAC
11/17/06	Yu Fen Huang	5000	Joe Biden PAC
11/17/06	Winkle Paw	2500	Joe Biden PAC
11/27/06	Stanley Lim	-400	Hillary Clinton
01/12/07	Winkle Paw	5000	HILLPAC
01/12/07	Yu Fen Huang	2100	Hillary Clinton
01/12/07	Yu Fen Huang	2100	Hillary Clinton
01/12/07	Danny Lee	2300	Hillary Clinton
01/12/07	Danny Lee	2300	Hillary Clinton
01/12/07	Normal Hsu	2100	Hillary Clinton
01/12/07	Normal Hsu	2100	Hillary Clinton
01/26/07	Su Paul	2100	Hillary Clinton
01/26/07	Su Paul	2100	Hillary Clinton
01/26/07	Yu Fen Huang	1900	Hillary Clinton
01/26/07	Yu Fen Huang	2300	Hillary Clinton
01/26/07	Danny Lee	1900	Hillary Clinton
01/26/07	Danny Lee	2300	Hillary Clinton
01/26/07	Norman Hsu	2100	Hillary Clinton
01/26/07	Norman Hsu	2100	Hillary Clinton
01/31/07	Danny Lee	10000	DSCC
01/31/07	Winkle Paw	10000	DSCC
01/31/07	Norman Hsu	5000	DSCC
02/02/07	Su Paul	200	Hillary Clinton
02/02/07	Su Paul	200	Hillary Clinton

02/02/07	Su Paul	3500	DSCC
02/02/07	Soe Lee	2300	Hillary Clinton
02/02/07	Soe Lee	2300	Hillary Clinton
02/02/07	Norman Hsu	200	Hillary Clinton
02/02/07	Norman Hsu	200	Hillary Clinton
02/09/07	Winkle Paw	5000	DNC
02/14/07	Soe Lee	1000	Kirsten Gillibrand
02/14/07	Danny Lee	2000	Kirsten Gillibrand
02/14/07	Norman Hsu	2300	Kirsten Gillibrand
02/14/07	Norman Hsu	2300	Kirsten Gillibrand
02/22/07	Su Paul	2300	Mary Landrieu
02/22/07	Yu Fen Huang	2000	Jay Rockefeller
02/22/07	Danny Lee	2000	Jay Rockefeller
02/22/07	Vivian Paw	2000	Jay Rockefeller
02/22/07	Marina Paw	2000	Jay Rockefeller
02/22/07	Winkle Paw	2000	Jay Rockefeller
02/22/07	Norman Hsu	2000	Jay Rockefeller
02/22/07	Norman Hsu	700	Mary Landrieu
02/22/07	Norman Hsu	2300	Mary Landrieu
02/22/07	Su Paul	200	Mary Landrieu
02/23/07	Yu Fen Huang	2300	Mary Landrieu
02/23/07	Danny Lee	2300	Mary Landrieu
02/23/07	Danny Lee	2300	Mary Landrieu
02/26/07	Yu Fen Huang	2300	Mary Landrieu
02/28/07	Su Paul	200	Jack Reed
02/28/07	Su Paul	2300	Jack Reed
02/28/07	Winkle Paw	2300	Jack Reed
02/28/07	Winkle Paw	2300	Jack Reed
02/28/07	Norman Hsu	200	Jack Reed
02/28/07	Norman Hsu	2300	Jack Reed
03/12/07	William Paw	2300	Tom Harkin
03/12/07	William Paw	2300	Tom Harkin
03/12/07	Soe Lee	2300	Tom Harkin
03/12/07	Soe Lee	2300	Tom Harkin
03/12/07	Yu Fen Huang	2300	Tom Harkin
03/12/07	Yu Fen Huang	2300	Tom Harkin

Date	Contributor	Amount	Recipient
03/12/07	Danny Lee	2300	Tom Harkin
03/12/07	Danny Lee	2300	Tom Harkin
03/12/07	Winkle Paw	2300	Tom Harkin
03/12/07	Winkle Paw	2300	Tom Harkin
03/12/07	Norman Hsu	2300	Tom Harkin
03/12/07	Norman Hsu	2300	Tom Harkin
03/14/07	Stanley Lim	2300	Hillary Clinton
03/14/07	Soe Lee	4600	Hillary Clinton
03/14/07	Yu Fen Huang	400	Hillary Clinton
03/14/07	Danny Lee	400	Hillary Clinton
03/14/07	Winkle Paw	2300	Hillary Clinton
03/14/07	Winkle Paw	2300	Hillary Clinton
03/15/07	Norman Hsu	1000	Thomas Allen
03/18/07	Su Paul	2300	Tom Harkin
03/18/07	Su Paul	2300	Tom Harkin
03/22/07	Norman Hsu	1000	Frank Lautenberg
03/27/07	Su Paul	500	Patrick Kennedy
03/27/07	Danny Lee	500	Patrick Kennedy
03/27/07	Norman Hsu	2500	DSCC
03/28/07	Su Paul	5000	Tom Allen
03/28/07	Danny Lee	500	Tom Allen
03/29/07	Vivian Paw	2300	Hillary Clinton
03/29/07	Vivian Paw	2300	Hillary Clinton
03/30/07	Norman Hsu	2300	Al Franken
03/31/07	Su Paul	10000	DCCC
03/31/07	Danny Lee	5000	DCCC
03/31/07	Winkle Paw	5000	DSCC
03/31/07	Norman Hsu	2000	David Loebsack
04/10/07	Norman Hsu	2000	Joe Sestak
04/12/07	Su Paul	1000	Joe Sestak
04/27/07	Danny Lee	250	Joe Sestak
04/27/07	Winkle Paw	500	Joe Sestak
04/28/07	Vivian Paw	2500	Ted Kennedy PAC
04/28/07	Marina Paw	2500	Ted Kennedy PAC
04/28/07	Winkle Paw	2500	Ted Kennedy PAC
04/28/07	Norman Hsu	5000	Ted Kennedy

Date	Name	Amount	Recipient
04/30/07	Soe Lee	-4600	Hillary Clinton
05/02/07	Soe Lee	2500	Ted Kennedy PAC
05/02/07	Yu Fen Huang	2500	Ted Kennedy PAC
05/02/07	Danny Lee	2500	Ted Kennedy PAC
05/03/07	Lelawattie Su	2300	Hillary Clinton
05/03/07	Lelawattie Su	2300	Hillary Clinton
05/03/07	Su Paul	500	Tom Vilsack
05/03/07	Su Paul	500	Tom Vilsack
05/03/07	Norman Hsu	2300	Tom Vilsack
05/03/07	Norman Hsu	200	Mark Pryor
05/03/07	Norman Hsu	2300	Mark Pryor
05/03/07	Alice Paw	2300	Hillary Clinton
05/03/07	Alice Paw	2300	Hillary Clinton
05/04/07	Danny Lee	200	Mark Pryor
05/04/07	Danny Lee	2300	Mark Pryor
05/04/07	Winkle Paw	2300	Mark Pryor
05/04/07	Winkle Paw	200	Mark Pryor
05/17/07	Su Paul	1000	Jay Rockefeller
05/18/07	Su Paul	1000	Patrick Murphy
05/18/07	Danny Lee	250	Patrick Murphy
05/23/07	Su Paul	1000	Mark Pryor
06/06/07	Su Paul	1000	Kirsten Gillibrand
06/06/07	Yu Fen Huang	2300	Kirsten Gillibrand
06/06/07	Vivian Paw	2300	Kirsten Gillibrand
06/06/07	Marina Paw	2300	Kirsten Gillibrand
06/06/07	Winkle Paw	2300	Kirsten Gillibrand
06/08/07	Vivian Paw	200	Mark Pryor
06/08/07	Vivian Paw	2300	Mark Pryor
06/08/07	Winkle Paw	700	Jay Rockefeller
06/08/07	Norman Hsu	300	Jay Rockefeller
06/08/07	Norman Hsu	1700	Jay Rockefeller

06/14/07	Vivian Paw	2300	Tom Harkin
06/14/07	Vivian Paw	2300	Tom Harkin
06/14/07	Marina Paw	2300	Tom Harkin
06/14/07	Marina Paw	2300	Tom Harkin
06/18/07	Yu Fen Huang	500	Tom Allen
06/25/07	William Paw	1000	Mike Honda
06/25/07	Vivian Paw	1000	Mike Honda
06/25/07	Norman Hsu	1000	Mark Udall
06/25/07	Norman Hsu	1000	Mike Honda
06/28/07	Winkle Paw	1000	Patrick Kennedy
06/28/07	Norman Hsu	1000	Patrick Kennedy